Global Security & Intelligence Studies

Also from Westphalia Press

westphaliapress.org

Global Security & Intelligence Studies

Volume 2, Number 2
Fall/Winter 2017

Melissa Schnyder, Editor

WESTPHALIA PRESS
An imprint of Policy Studies Organization

Global Security and Intelligence Studies: Volume 2, Number 2, Fall/Winter 2017
All Rights Reserved © 2017 by Policy Studies Organization

Westphalia Press
An imprint of Policy Studies Organization
1527 New Hampshire Ave., NW
Washington, D.C. 20036
info@ipsonet.org

ISBN-13: 978-1-63391-620-3
ISBN-10: 1-63391-620-0

Cover design by Jeffrey Barnes:
jbarnesbook.design

Daniel Gutierrez-Sandoval, Executive Director
PSO and Westphalia Press

Updated material and comments on this edition
can be found at the Westphalia Press website:
www.westphaliapress.org

TABLE OF CONTENTS

Editorial Welcome

Global Security and Intelligence Studies aims to publish high-quality and original research on contemporary security and intelligence issues. The journal is committed to methodological pluralism, and seeks to help bridge the gap between scholars and practitioners engaged in security and intelligence issues by publishing rigorous research, book reviews, and reflections on the field that are relevant to both communities. We will, on occasion, also seek to publish special issues on timely intelligence and security topics, and welcome proposals that fit with the scope and aims of the journal. The journal actively encourages both former and current intelligence and security practitioners to participate in important scholarly and policy debate, and invites them to contribute their research to the journal. As a result, we hope that the journal will become a vibrant platform for informed, reasoned, and relevant debates on the most important intelligence and security issues of our time.

As we publish the most recent issue, there are many exciting changes occurring with GSIS. First, I would like to take this opportunity to introduce myself as the new editor of GSIS. I am excited and honored to take on this role and continue advancing the work of the journal in the areas of readership, author submissions, and the editorial board. I would like to thank the former editors, Yoav Gortzak and Patricia J. Campbell, for their service and contributions to the journal.

We have restructured the journal to include sections that highlight research, practice, and more. In addition to continuing the Articles and Book Review sections, we have added a Voices from the Field section to provide a forum for discussion about contemporary global security and intelligence issues. We are also working on adding an Emerging Scholars section so that the editorial board can work with advanced Master's and doctoral students to disseminate their research in an effort to provide additional support, guidance, and an opportunity to publish.

Although GSIS accepts submissions year-round, due dates have been established for the new release schedule. We are moving from a Spring and Fall issue publication schedule to a Spring/Summer issue with a February 1 deadline, followed by a Fall/Winter issue with an August 1 deadline.

The articles in this issue of GSIS address a number of important topics in focusing on the theme of challenges and opportunities of teaching intelligence analysis. In *Teaching the Millennial Intelligence Analyst*, Margaret S. Marangione examines the millennial generation and their unique challenges as students and intelligence analysts, and explores how teaching methods and coursework can be crafted to meet the specific learning styles characteristics of millennials.

In *Teaching the Intelligence Collection Disciplines: The Effectiveness of Experiential Learning as a Pedagogical Technique*, Keith Cozine examines experiential learning techniques in intelligence collection projects that require students to utilize open sources, human sources, and geospatial sources with the aim of addressing challenges related to teaching intelligence collection. Finally, in *Peer Review Skill Development in Intelligence Education*, John Andrews and Dale Nute examine the benefits of peer review for critical analysis and collaboration among students in the intelligence field.

An invited article is included in this issue's inaugural Voices from the Field section. In *Teaching Intelligence Analysis: An Academic and Practitioner Discussion*, Richard J. Kilroy, Jr. summarizes a roundtable discussion that took place at the May 23, 2017 International Association for Intelligence Education (IAFIE) Conference in Charles Town, West Virginia. The roundtable participants included faculty members from five universities in the United States who shared their views on how they approach the teaching of intelligence analysis within their specific academic departments and disciplines.

Lastly, three book reviews are presented. Rhys Ball provides a review of Sean Naylor's book, *Relentless Strike: The Secret History of Joint Special Operations Command*; Clinton L. Ervin reviews Paul R. Pillar's book, *Why America Misunderstands the World: National Experience and Roots of Misperception*; and, finally, João Estevens reviews *The Handbook of European Intelligence Cultures*, edited by Bob de Graaff and James N. Nyce, with Chelsea Locke.

Publishing an academic journal is a collaborative process. We would like to extend our gratitude to the authors, to our peer reviewers for their feedback and commitment, and the members of the editorial board for their support and input.

On behalf of the editorial team,

Melissa Schnyder
American Public University System

lobal Security and Intelligence Studies busca publicar investigación de alta calidad y original acerca de temas contemporáneos de seguridad e inteligencia. La revista está comprometida con el pluralismo metodológico, y busca ayudar a cerrar la brecha entre los académicos y los involucrados en seguridad y temas de inteligencia al publicar investigación rigurosa, reseñas de libros y reflexiones del tema que son relevantes para ambas comunidades. También, ocasionalmente, buscaremos publicar ediciones especiales acerca de los temas de inteligencia y seguridad recientes, y acogemos propuestas que quepan dentro de la envergadura y objetivos de la revista. La revista fomenta activamente tanto a los profesionales de la inteligencia anteriores, como a los contemporáneos para participar en un importante debate académico y político, y los invita a contribuir sus investigaciones a la revista. Como resultado, esperamos que la revista se convierta en una plataforma dinámica para debates informados, fundamentados y relevantes acerca de los problemas más importantes de inteligencia y seguridad de nuestra época.

En lo que publicamos nuestra más reciente edición, hay muchos cambios emocionantes que están ocurriendo en GSIS. Primero, me gustaría tomar esta oportunidad para presentarme como nuevo editor de GSIS. Me emociona y estoy honrado de desempeñarme en esta calidad y continuar el trabajo de la revista en las áreas del público, contribuciones y la junta editorial. Me gustaría agradecer a los editores anteriores, Yoav Gortzak y Patricia J. Campbell, por su servicio y contribuciones a la revista.

Hemos cambiado la estructura de la revista para poder incluir secciones que resaltan la investigación, la práctica, y mucho más. Además de continuar con las secciones de Artículos y Reseñas de Libros, hemos también añadido una sección de Voces del Campo para proporcionar un foro para discutir los problemas mundiales y contemporáneos de la seguridad e inteligencia. También estamos trabajando para incluir una sección de académicos emergentes para que la junta editorial pueda trabajar con estudiantes avanzados de maestría y doctorado para difundir sus investigaciones en un esfuerzo para proporcionar apoyo adicional, orientación y una oportunidad de publicar.

GSIS acepta contribuciones todo el año, pero también ya se han establecido nuevas fechas límite para la nueva lista de publicación. Nos estamos cambiando de una lista de publicación de primavera y otoño a una edición primavera/verano con una fecha límite del primero de febrero, seguida por una edición de otoño/invierno con fecha límite del primero de agosto.

Los artículos en esta edición de GSIS abordan un número de temas importantes al enfocarse en el tema de los retos y oportunidades de enseñar el análisis de inteligencia. En *Enseñar a analistas de inteligencia de la generación milenial*, Margaret S. Marangione examina la generación milenial y sus retos únicos como estudiantes y analistas de inteligencia, y explora cómo los métodos de enseñanza y materiales didácticos pueden ser diseñados para estilos específicos de aprendiza-je para las características de la generación milenial. En *Enseñar las disciplinas de recopilación de inteligencia: La efectividad del aprendizaje experimental como una técnica pedagógica,* Keith Cozine examina las técnicas de aprendizaje experiencial en proyectos de recopilación de inteligencia que requieren que los estudiantes uti-licen fuentes abiertas, recursos humanos y recursos geoespaciales para resolver retos de la enseñanza de recopilación de inteligencia. Finalmente, en *Desarrollo de habilidades de revisión en pares para la educación de inteligencia,* John Andrews y Dale Nute examinan los beneficios de la revisión por pares para el análisis crítico y la colaboración entre estudiantes en el campo de la inteligencia.

Se incluye un artículo invitado en la nueva sección de Voces del Campo de esta edición. En *Enseñanza del análisis de inteligencia: Una discusión académica y práctica,* Richard J. Kilroy, Jr. resume una discusión de mesa redonda que tuvo tugar en la conferencia de la International Association for Intelligence Education (IAFIE) el 23 de mayo de 2017 en Charles Town, Virginia Occidental. Los partici-pantes de la mesa redonda incluían miembros del profesorado de cinco universi-dades en los Estados Unidos que compartieron sus puntos de vista de qué métodos utilizar para la enseñanza del análisis de inteligencia dentro de sus departamentos académicos y disciplinas específicas.

Por último, se presentan tres reseñas de libros. Rhys Ball aporta una reseña del libro de San Naylor, *Relentless Strike: La historia secreta del comando de op-eraciones especiales conjunto;* Clinton L. Ervin reseña el libro de Paul R. Pillar *Por qué EE. UU. no entiende al mundo: la falsa percepción de la experiencia nacional y las raíces;* y finalmente, João Estevens reseña el *Manual de culturas de inteligencia europeas,* editado por Bob de Graaff y James N. Nyce, con Chelsea Locke.

Publicar una revista académica es un proceso colaborativo. Nos gustaría dar las gracias a los autores, a nuestros revisores por su retroalimentación y comprom-iso y a los miembros de la junta editorial por su apoyo y contribuciones.

De parte del equipo de edición,

Melissa Schnyder
American Public University System

"全球安全和情报研究"（Global Security and Intelligence Studies，简称 GSIS）期刊致力发表有关当代安全和情报问题的高质量原创研究。期刊使用方法论多元主义（methodological pluralism），同时通过发表严谨的科学研究、书评和相关学者及从业人员对安全和情报问题的看法，进而试图缩小学者和从业人员在此问题上的观念差距。有时，我们也会争取发表有关及时情报和安全话题的特刊，并欢迎适合本期刊范围和宗旨的不同提议。不论是曾经从事过情报安全的人员，还是在职者，期刊都鼓励二者参与重要的学术和政策辩论，并邀请他们投稿。最终，我们希望期刊能成为一个活跃的平台，为当下首要情报和安全问题提供有知识、有逻辑的相关辩论。

出版最近一期文章的同时，GSIS也发生了许多令人兴奋的变化。首先，我想借此机会介绍自己成为GSIS的一名新编辑。能担当这一角色，我感到既兴奋又荣幸。我将继续促进期刊工作（包括读者、作者投稿和编辑委员会）的进行。我想感谢前编辑Yoav Gortzak和Patricia J. Campbell，她们都为期刊做出了应有的努力和贡献。

我们对期刊进行了重建，加入了不同板块，这些板块强调研究和实践等内容。在继续保留文章和书评（Articles and Book Review）部分的同时，我们增添了"领域之声"（Voices from the Field ）板块，为有关当代全球安全和情报问题的讨论提供了论坛。我们还将添加"青年学者"（Emerging Scholars）板块，帮助编辑委员会和杰出硕士及博士生一同合作，传播研究，以提供额外支持、指导以及发表文章的机会。

尽管GSIS全年都接受投稿，新的时间表已确定了投稿截止日。之前的春季和秋季期刊发行时间改为了春夏和秋冬两期，截止日分别为2月1日和8月1日。

本期文章处理了一系列重要话题，这些话题都聚焦于情报分析教学的机遇和挑战。在文章"教授千禧一代的情报分析师"(*Teaching the Millennial Intelligence Analyst*)中，Margaret S. Marangione博士检验了千禧一代和他们作为学生及情报分析师面临的独特挑战，同时探索了教学方式和课程作业如何经过有技巧的调整，达到符合千禧一代的特定学习方式。在另一篇文章"情报收集类别的教学：体验式学习作为一种教学技巧的有效性"（*Teaching the Intelligence Collection Disciplines: The Effectiveness of Experiential Learning as a Pedagogical Technique*）中，Keith Cozine博士检验了情报收集项目中体验式学习技巧的使用。情报收集项目要求学生使用公开来源（open sources）、人力来源(human sources)和地理空间来源(geospatial sources)，解决情报收集教学的相关挑战。在最后一篇文章"情报教育中同行评审的技能发展"（*Peer Review Skill Development in Intelligence Education*）中，John Andrews 和Dale Nute博士检验了情报界学生进行批判分析和协作时使用同行评审的益处。

本期首次推出的"领域之声"板块包含一篇特邀文章，名为"大学教师和从业人员对情报分析教学的讨论"（*Teaching Intelligence Analysis: An Academic and Practitioner Discussion*）。在这篇文章中，Richard J. Kilroy, Jr.博士对一次圆桌讨论进行了总结。该讨论在美国西弗吉尼亚查尔斯镇举办的国际情报教育协会（International Associate for Intelligence Education，简称IAFIE）会议中完成。参加圆桌讨论的学者分别来自美国的5所大学，他们分享了各自如何在其特定的学术部门和学科下进行情报分析教学。

期刊最后呈现了三篇书评。Rhys Ball评论了肖恩·内勒（Sean Naylor）著作《无情打击：联合特种作战司令部的秘密历史》（*Relentless Strike: The Secret History of Joint Special Operations Command*）；Clinton L. Ervin评论了保罗·R. 皮勒（Paul R. Pillar）著作《美国为何误解世界：国家经历和误解根源》（*Why America Misunderstands the World: National Experience and Roots of Misperception*）；João Estevens评论了由 Bob de Graaff、James N. Nyce和Chelsea Locke共同编辑的《欧洲情报文化手册》（*The Handbook of European Intelligence Cultures*）。

发表学术期刊是一个协作过程。我们对作者表示衷心感谢，同时也感谢同行评审员的反馈和投入，以及编辑委员会成员的支持。

谨代表编辑组，

Melissa Schnyder

美国公立大学系统

Teaching the Millennial Intelligence Analyst

Margaret S. Marangione[1]

ABSTRACT

This paper examines the conclusions of researchers regarding the millennial generation and their unique challenges as students and intelligence analysts (IAs), and determines that a carefully crafted framework of coursework can be correlated and a curriculum built to the core competencies of ICD 610, as well as take into account the unique variables of millennial intelligence analysts and the needs of the intelligence community. By examining the paradigm shifts of the intelligence community, the demographic of the millennial population and current and future educational trends, this paper argues that teaching methods and competency coursework must be adapted and designed to meet millennials' specific learning styles. Unless coursework is designed for the needs of this population, millennial IAs will not be able to build on their present skills or enhance their expertise. Government, education institutions and contractors must examine how they will authentically assess IA learning to meet the ICD 610 skill set. By readapting intelligence curricula, building in clear assessment, flipping the classroom as well as mapping learning outcomes back to ICD 610, a concrete framework can be provided for delivering to the government excellent service through measurable skill training education.

Keywords: intelligence education, intelligence collection, intelligence training, tradecraft, millennials.

RESUMEN

Este documento examina las conclusiones de los investigadores que investigan la generación milenial y sus retos únicos como estudiantes y analistas de inteligencia (IAs), y determina que un marco de estudios cuidadosamente diseñado puede estar relacionado con

1   Syntelligent Analytic Solutions, LLC
    200 Little Falls Street, Suite 407, Falls Church, VA 22046, USA
    Phone: 540.736.4570. Email: Margaret.marangione@syntelligent.com

un currículum hecho con las competencias básicas de ICD 610, así como tomar en cuenta las variables únicas de los analistas de inteligencia de la generación milenial y las necesidades de la comunidad de inteligencia. Al examinar estos cambios de paradigma de la comunidad de inteligencia, la demografía de la población milenial y las tendencias educativas futuras, este artículo argumenta que los métodos de enseñanza y contenido para enseñar las competencias debe ser adaptado y designado para concordar con los estilos particulares de aprendizaje de la generación milenial. A menos que las clases estén diseñadas para las necesidades de esta población, los analistas de inteligencia de la generación milenial no podrán continuar desarrollando sus habilidades o mejorando su experiencia. El gobierno, las instituciones educativas y los contratistas deben examinar cómo van a evaluar auténticamente el aprendizaje de los analistas de inteligencia para aprender las habilidades de ICD 610. Al readaptar el currículum e incluir una evaluación clara, cambiando los salones de clase y también esquematizar los resultados del aprendizaje de vuelta a ICD 610, un marco concreto puede ser proporcionado al servicio excelente del gobierno a través de la educación de entrenamiento de habilidades medibles.

Palabras clave: *educación de inteligencia, recopilación de inteligencia, entrenamiento de inteligencia, oficio, generación milenial*

摘要

本文检验了情报研究者对千禧一代和后者作为学生及情报分析师（intelligence analysts, 简称IAs）所面临的独特挑战得出的结果；同时确定了一项严密制作的课程作业框架，该框架能和美国情报界第610号指令"情报界工作人员胜任能力目录"（简称ICD 610）中的核心能力素质（core competencies）相联系，同时还会将千禧一代IAs特有的可变因素以及情报界的需求考虑在内。通过检查有关情报界、千禧一代人口统计数据、现下和未来教育趋势的范式转变，本文主张，情报教学方法和能力课程作业必须作出调整，以符合千禧一代的特定学习方式。如果课程作业没有按照千禧一代的需求进行设计，则这一代的IAs将不能获得现有技能，或是提高其专业水平。政府、教育机构和承包商必须检查各自将如何真正评估IA为达到ICD610技能所付出的学习情况。通过重新调整情报课程、建立明确评估、翻转课堂和将学习结果反映到ICD610中，则能提供一个使用可测量技能培训教育的具体框架，为政府带来优质服务。

关键词：情报教育，情报收集，情报训练，谍报技术，千禧一代

Introduction

Increasingly, in a highly competitive market, employers want to be able to confirm that employees meet a baseline of core competencies. In the twenty-first century both the education community and the intelligence community have been forced to evaluate objectives, assessments, and outcomes especially when it comes to productivity of students or employees; the twenty-first century is an accountability climate and bureaucracies have found that outlining core competencies provides a baseline of expected proficiency. Just like academia, the intelligence community must transmit and preserve the wisdom developed in the past while anticipating future anticipated knowledge, skills, and behaviors. The transmission of past culture is an easier task than forecasting the future with a crystal ball and as a result students and intelligence analysts may not be prepared to deal with the requirements of a future society based on a changing paradigm of non-state actors, traditional teaching techniques, and a millennial skill base. Furthermore, accessing, measuring, and integrating assurance quality with intelligence community directive (ICD) critical competencies is not easy or simple. This is further complicated by the current workforce, the Millennial Generation. This a generation that approaches learning and employment with decidedly different values than any previous generation and may not bring the critical thinking skill set that an older generation values to their jobs.

In the twenty-first century, our culture has had profound economic, demographic, social, and intelligence upheavals, which has impacted every aspect of society to include the new generation of students and analysts. What cuts across disciplines is the powerful revolution of the information age. Because of these transformations, most institutions have been forced to restructure to meet an ever changing environment. The education system began this journey with the standards of learning (SOL) in the late twentieth century and in most institutions of higher learning, online classes, smart classrooms, and flipped classroom models have had to be adopted, adapted, and addressed to meet the technology changes and learners who came of age with smartphones and the Internet. Just like the education community had to realign, the intelligence community galvanized after the cognitive dissonance of 9/11, resulting in first, a values shift, and then ideology development with the Director of National Intelligence (DNI) and the skill development outlined in ICD 610. By clearly identifying a benchmark of the core competencies of an intelligence analyst's skill set, the government has set the training standard for intelligence education professionals as well as contractors striving to provide the government with expert analysts.

But a model for change requires behavioral change. Sociocultural behavioral learning theories, skill development, training of staff or students, and a platform for that skill development must be integrated for a student, employee, or organization to change. Meeting (and educating to) these skill needs of the core competencies are not that straightforward. It can be assumed that individuals with at least two years of college experience have been provided some experience in critical thinking and writing. By completion of a four-year degree program, most students have also been exposed to critical thinking methodologies. But do intelligence analysts formally apply critical thinking methodologies, except when management forces them to do so? Can employer-required coursework help IAs to develop more logical approaches to deal with problems in their IC jobs? Do courses need to be built and designed around IAs' specific challenges and needs? And finally, have course developers or educators taken into account the documented differences of the millennial generation's learning style to effectively reach and train them?

This paper examines the conclusions of researchers regarding the millennial generation and their unique challenges as students and IAs, and determines that a carefully crafted framework of coursework can be correlated and a curriculum built to the core competencies of ICD 610 while taking into account the unique variables of millennial intelligence analysts and the needs of the intelligence community. By examining the paradigm shifts of the intelligence community, the demographics of the millennial population, and current and future educational trends, this paper argues that teaching methods and competency coursework must be adapted and designed to meet millennials' specific learning styles. Unless coursework is designed for the needs of this population, millennial IAs will not be able to build on their present skills or enhance their expertise. Government, education institutions, and contractors must examine how they will authentically assess IA learning to meet the ICD 610 skill set. By readapting intelligence curricula, building in clear assessment, flipping the classroom as well as mapping learning outcomes back to ICD 610, a concrete framework can be provided for delivering to the government excellent service through measurable skill training education.

The Challenges

The Intelligence Community

The intelligence community has had a long standing debate on whether intelligence analysis is a craft or profession, and this may have fueled the current educational challenges of preparing the millennial generation for careers as intelligence analysts. Also, there have been issues with the intelligence community both in training and framework, which had begun to be voiced by intelligence experts as early as the 1990s, with a movement toward intelligence reform after 9/11. Robert Johnston's (2005) book, *Analytic Culture in the U.S Intelligence Community*, funded by the Central Intelligence Agency's Center for the Study of Intelligence, offers conclusions that are not what many in the world of intelligence analysis would like to hear. His findings constitute not just a strong indictment of the way American intelligence performs analysis, but also, a guide for how to do better. Johnston finds no baseline standard analytic method. Instead, the most common practice is to conduct limited brainstorming on the basis of previous analysis, thus producing a bias toward confirming earlier views. The validating of data is questionable—for instance, the directorate of operations (DO) cleaning of spy reports does not permit testing of their validity—reinforcing the tendency to look for data that confirms, not refutes, prevailing hypotheses. The process is risk averse, with considerable managerial conservatism. There is much more emphasis on avoiding error than on imagining surprises. He also finds that the analytic process is driven by current intelligence, especially the CIA's analytic product, the President's Daily Brief (PDB), which, Johnston caricatured as "CNN plus secrets." The intelligence community does more reporting than in-depth analysis because of the current structure of the community.

One of the solutions to fix the hole in the dyke was the Intelligence Reform and Terrorism Prevention Act of 2004 (IRTPA), which created, among other things, the Director of National Intelligence (DNI), and established goals of information sharing and analytic standards to include ICD 203 and ICD 610. These requirements have forced tradecraft to take a long, hard look at the current skill base needed for IAs, the gaps in the education process, the implications of training in a new and evolving tradecraft paradigm and recently and importantly, the implications of millennials as future IAs.

While ICD 203 and ICD 610 clearly spell out the hard and soft skills needed for a twenty-first century intelligence community and analyst, ICD 203 outlines the core principles, assessment criteria, and product valuation with the goal of providing "academic rigor and excellence and for personal integrity in analytic practice." ICD 610 definitively captures the core competencies needed for the GS-15 intelligence community for civilian employees. These ground breaking initiatives have come at a time when U.S. experts and agencies, post 9/11, expressed the sentiment that analytical capabilities, and human and technical procedures, were in need of repair, replacement, and overhaul in order to be able to be responsive to the nature of twenty-first century threats. Additionally, the Intelligence Education Community has been in a debate about the role of training, education, and the foundation of social science methodology in bridging the gap from graduate to government analyst, which has been mapped in Landon-Murray and Coulthart (2016).

Graduate to Government Analyst

All of these issues come at a time when colleges and the workforce are composed heavily of the millennial generation, a generation that has significantly different values and engagement with education and work (Schweitzer 2010). This occurs alongside data that points to millennials' weaknesses in a hard and soft skill base regardless of whether or not they have a four-year degree. For example, researchers at the Princeton-based Educational Testing Service (ETS) administered students a test called the Program for the International Assessment of Adult Competencies (PIAAC) (2017). The test was designed to measure the job skills of adults, aged 16–65, in 23 countries. When the results were analyzed by age group and nationality, data showed that millennials in the United States fall short when it comes to the skills employers want most: literacy, (including the ability to follow simple instructions), practical math, and "problem-solving in technology-rich environments" (Princeton University 2017). Also, in a 2015 Future Workforce Report, 60 percent of managers polled felt millennials lacked critical thinking and problem-solving skills, 50 percent felt they lacked attention to detail, and 44 percent stated they lacked leadership skills as well (*The Economist* 2017).

Millennials, Higher Education, and the ICD Standards

For college faculty, this generation can also be a challenging one to deal with and while there are many popular articles about the millennial attitude, the following summary from Neilson (2010) provides a solid overview. Millennials view higher education as an expensive but economically necessary consumer good, not a goal that is fueled by hard work and outstanding performance (Neilson 2010). They (or their parents) "purchase" it for the purpose of opening well-paying occupational doors on graduation, so they feel entitled to their degree for the cost of the credits (Neilson 2010).

Many of them were subjected to the rote memorization for SOLs and therefore are not prepared for college inquiry, meta-analysis, and synthesis of information. Critical thinking, the ability to synthesize information, and meta-analysis are not skill bases developed by multiple choice and memorization. Instead, high-impact learning practices include, but are not limited to: common learning experiences, writing intensive courses, collaborative projects, and global learning (Stellar 2017, 220). These practices engage the student in real-world learning that mirrors what the external world of work will demand from them. As Dr. James Stellar (2017, 220) eloquently stated "... college students respond and grow because they are using both their hearts and their heads." Learning theories demonstrates for the millennial learner engagement, both at work and school, relevancy, immediacy and collaboration. For example, the principles of Tokuhama-Espinosa's (2014) work are shaped by the ideas that every student and brain is unique and molded by past experiences. This is particularly relevant for the millennial learner, whose past experiences have been shaped by the political, economic, and social challenges of the twenty-first century (Tokuhama-Espinosa 2014).

As the case studies in Tapscott (2010) showcase, millennials resent the amount of reading, research, problem solving, and writing that is assigned them and the standards that are held for their work. Because millennials are a generation marked by fragility, those whose grades slip feel their self-esteem threatened and may react with depression, anxiety, defensiveness, and even anger against professors. Additionally, they need trigger warnings and safe spaces if their belief and value systems are questioned (Tapscott 2010).

Also, because of their exposure to digital media and other cultural influences, they do not respond to courses that are conventionally delivered through online or seated classroom structures and have a traditional course format—lecture, read, respond, or test. A question that must be addressed by trainers and educators is how to get millennials to buy into course work that is mostly static and traditional (e.g., lecture) and may not take into account how the millennial generation learns or what they value.

Even though writing (along with soft skills) has been clearly documented as a challenge by the workforce and educators, the ICD mandates are mainly concerned with analytic standards which proscribe "the production and evaluation of analytic products" (Tapscott 2010). The Analytic Tradecraft Standards specifically address research, methodology, evaluation, assumptions, alternatives, implications, logic, accuracy, and visual layout but only briefly refer to actual writing as in standard 3: "Language and syntax should convey meaning unambiguously" (ICD 203, 4). All of the nine ICD 203 Standards specifically outline research and analysis, and most research and analysis courses provide basic coverage outlined in the requirements of the standards. It is also feasible to develop courses that will encompass analysis of competing hypothesis principles, risk assessments, probability, scenario analysis, etc. To further prepare our students, colleges as well as technical schools like the Intelligence and Security Academy, also offer technical writing classes along with research methods and analysis. But, even with these courses at their fingertips, graduates may not be competent to meet the basic IA skill set upon graduation. Moreover, most of the coursework has not incorporated social behavioral learning theories and how millennials learn into course delivery.

The Millennial Generation

Even with the best course work and constructed classes all aligned to the ICD 203 Analytic Standards, educators and employers must take into account the current students and next generation of IAs if we are going to bridge the gap from graduate to competent employee. Understanding them is the first step, and that comes with the definition of who they are. Millennials are defined as people born from 1980 to 2004. There are over 73 million young adults currently aged 18–34. Some of them are now in elected and staff positions in Congress and fill essential positions with contractors, as well as jobs across all 17 intelligence agencies. Simply put, they are on the receiving end of the intelligence and are analyzing and driving its collection; they fill the seats in our classrooms (Weinbaum, Richard, and Jenny 2016).

Culturally, they have had major social, political, and economic issues on their radar screen. They have always lived with the threat of school shootings or violence, like the Ohio University shootings, Columbine, Sandy Hook, Virginia Tech, and the recent hate crimes demonstrated in Charlottesville, Virginia. They have witnessed the worst of corporate greed in the Enron fraud, watched the controversy of the Snowden leaks and the divisive presidential election and presidency. The current political circus has fortified their already shaky faith in the government and the political system. In 2014, only 20 percent of millennials polled trusted the federal government and only 22 percent were sure that Snowden jeopardized national security (Weinbaum, Richard, and Jenny 2016, 12–15). They are conflicted over their personal experience with SOL testing and the reality about student loan debt (an average of $45,000 per student) (Weinbaum, Richard, and Jenny 2016, 12–15). The challenge of finding gainful employment and the unclear certainty that an educational degree actually brings success has millennials questioning the educational system's relevancy and approach to teaching them.

While we cannot change what has shaped them, we can be aware of what makes them tick. Some of the characteristics of millennials captured by researchers distinguish them as community-conscious, team-oriented, optimistic, sheltered, connected 24/7, and adopting technology as a way of life. What defines this generation apart from every previous generation that has come before it is that they have been raised in an environment of continuous exposure to digital media and this has shaped their perspective, use of that media, and how they evaluate what information they think of as timely or relevant. According to Oblinger (2003), to millennials computers are not considered a technology but are a way of life, and the Internet is preferable to the television; this technology affects what they perceive as real. Doing is more important than knowing and learning more closely resembles Nintendo rather than logic (Oblinger 2003).

Additionally, a profile of the millennial college student can include, as described in Rue (2002), exposure to vast information but less depth of it; high levels of stress and anxiety; learning disabilities and fragility; lack of study skills; ambitious but unrealistic expectations; lack of engagement in class participation; and becoming easily bored. Based on numerous sociocultural learning theories that explain thinking, brain development and how it correlates to learning, we are what we have been exposed to; the millennial student's brain is wired differently and their thinking patterns may have been changed through constant exposure to technology and media (Weinbaum, Richard, and Jenny 2016).

They are also a generation that has embraced tattoos and body piercings, and 69 percent believe marijuana should be legal (Weinbaum, Richard, and Jenny 2016, 30). Interestingly, this new generation has even influenced former Defense Secretary Ash Carter who announced a wide-ranging review of recruiting standards and practices to ensure they are not "unnecessarily restrictive." The possible changes, outlined in a fact sheet distributed by the military, include a review of policies governing past marijuana use, tattoos, single parenthood, and physical fitness standards (Reyes 2016).

Millennials and Media and Skills

As we know, mobile phones are the most important technological device in the lives of millennials. Pew researchers suggest that millennials treat their phone multitasking like body parts, for better or worse (Rainie and Zickuhr 2015). More than 8 in 10 millennials polled said they sleep with a cell phone glowing by the bed (Rainie and Zickuhr 2015). Because of this adaptation to technology, "They prefer quick responses to questions, have a sense of immediacy, and are impatient with the slow pace or organizations that are less than cutting edge in their usage of technology" (Rainie and Zickuhr 2015, 4). On a positive note, they want to share and discuss information and have an innate openness to change. These are significant factors for new training and educational course design because their attitude is not conducive to traditional lecture presentation of material. For college course development, initial buy-in and a smooth onboarding is critical for millennials. So, discussion of assessments, objectives, and value of learning tools can provide students with a shared understanding and possibly some agreement about skill-based validity and importance of course objectives.

The implications for faculty are to shift from thinking that their students are not interested, or worse yet, bored, to utilizing teaching approaches that will engage the millennial learner while building on the neuroscience models of learning. Collaborative research activities take into account the Community of Practice, that learning is social and that it is a skill that can be acquired. The Kolb Model of classroom activities builds on millennials' desire for interconnection and immediacy (Svinicki 1987, 141–146). First, learning is central to human identity and is a social motivation, which is why student learning can be facilitated by group work and team teaching. Self-directed research projects or activities may provide buy-in that millennials value and take in the first ideas of Community of Practice: what do they value? Allowing them to scaffold research activities individually as well as with a team allows each student to develop expert knowledge in a specific area. Allowing each team to teach by presenting their material to the class, as well as designing an assessment activity for their classmates, may help them develop and become aware of appropriate learning, studying and college behavior and hard and soft professional skills. This directly correlates to their marketability and skills they will need as employees.

Experiential learning activities (Kolb et al. 2001) provide excellent foundational activities for developing and facilitating learning. Also, the activities support and are conducive to the millennial learner who needs a hands-on and interactive approach instead of the traditional auditory lecture and retrieval testing (Kolb et al. 2001). Activities and assignments that demonstrate and encompass concrete experience (e.g., research and group work), reflective observation (e.g., writing), abstract conceptualization (e.g., artistic project), and active experimentation (e.g., team teaching) can provide the multiplatform experience that millennials need to be engaged. According to the National Training Laboratories report, students' attention average from lecture is 5 percent, from reading is 10 percent, from group discussion is 50 percent, then reaches 75 percent by doing, and 90 percent when a student experiments in a teaching role (Rivera 2016).

Additionally, these projects attempt to make the information "stick" by requiring students to solve and understand a problem, develop foundational knowledge through research and presentation of materials, elaborate by expressing ideas and concepts in their own words and make connections about what they know and how it relates to prior knowledge or experiences. As stated by Brown, Roedriger, and McDaniel (2014), "People who learn to extract key ideas from new material and organize [it] into a mental model and connect that model to prior knowledge show an advantage in learning complex mastery." Ultimately, this flips the classroom and makes the student the actor instead of the receiver of information and builds on the millennials' need for connectivity, authentic learning, and diversity of learning experiences.

Intelligence Analysis and Learning

Undoubtedly, millennials can be viewed as a challenge and flipping the classroom is not an easy feat. Certainly, higher education cannot do away with lecture and reading because the millennial generation simply does not like it or was not exposed to it, and this would have horrifying implications in the workforce, let alone the intelligence community that relies on intelligence analysts who must synthesize complex information. For example, analysts might need to consider social, military, economic, political, governmental, scientific, and technical issues surrounding an event or location. Additional challenges for an IA include training for avoiding analytical pitfalls like group think, risk aversion, preconceptions, etc.

Intelligence analysis illuminates information into a value added product and often deals with ambiguous situations that combine qualitative and quantitative research skills. Heuer (1991) details these points, as well as how human minds are not wired to cope effectively with both inherent and induced uncertainty. In addition, increased knowledge of our inherent biases tends to be of little assistance to the analyst, but tools and techniques that apply higher levels of critical thinking can substantially improve analysis on complex problems. In essence, one's perceptions are morphed by a variety of factors that are completely out of the control of the analyst. Heuer (1991) sees mental models as potentially good and bad for the analyst. On the positive side, they tend to simplify information for the sake of comprehension, but they also obscure genuine clarity of interpretation. Therefore, since all people observe the same information with inherent and different biases, Heuer believes an effective analysis system needs a few safeguards. It should encourage products that clearly show the assumptions and chains of inferences, and it should emphasize procedures that expose alternative points of view, an idea that has been incorporated into ICD 203. What is required of analysts is "a commitment to challenge, refine, and challenge again their own working mental models" (Heuer 1991). But how do we challenge millennials, improve their analytic capabilities and ability to synthesize information when they do not read?

Millennials and Learning

If you Google: "Do millennials read?," many articles from the Huffington Post to CBS news will state that millennials read more than any previous generation. Good news? Not quite. What millennials call reading, another generation might refer to as scanning. Based on information from Millennial Marketing, this is what some millennials had to say about books and reading:

> Even if I had the money to buy every textbook I ever needed in college, most of them would have collected dust on my shelves all semester ... part of my complete disinterest in textbooks comes from the fact that the second a book is published today, it is pretty much obsolete ... Furthermore, this online information is free or if it's not free, I'll go look on another site until I find it for free.

In May of 2009, I graduated from The University of North Carolina at Chapel Hill, a school consistently ranked as one of the best public universities in the country, and never checked out a single book.

Whether it is online or print, millennials do still read, but they read differently. Because they are reading for information, they are good scanners. In his book, Tapscott (2010) describes Joe O'Shea, a 22-year old student leader from Florida State who was on his way to study at Oxford; O'Shea had this to say about reading books:

> I don't read books per se, I go to Google and I can absorb relevant information quickly. Some of this comes from books but sitting down and going through a book from cover to cover doesn't make sense. It's not a good use of my time as I can get all the information I need faster through the Web. You need to know how to do it—to be a skilled hunter.

Earlier in his book, Tapscott (2010) spends several pages describing how and why millennials developed such scanning skills and explains how this ability may provide them with the broader frame of reference needed to be more sophisticated readers:

> The Net Gen brain may be able to execute certain perceptual tasks more rapidly, and may maintain more items in working memory. In order to deal with all that incoming information, you have to be a great scanner. Digital immersion has given the Net Generation the visual skills that make them superior scanners. They've learned to develop the filters they need to sort out what's important from what's not.

Millennials' habit of scanning, and of reading with purpose, may be good news for the intelligence community because it is a skill that can be utilized for scanning the huge amount of open source intelligence (OSINT) since key words, Twitter trending topics and other tools provide gateways into relevant content. Millennials have never experienced a day without Twitter, the Internet, Instagram, Snapchat, or Pinterest. They conduct research by going online and linking to source documentation and they monitor their every activity with Fitbit and Apple Watch. When they enter the intelligence workspace, they are radically underwhelmed by available tools, techniques, and processes. For example, newsworthy events are often posted, discussed, and dissected on Twitter before they are even detected in more traditional ways as is exemplified by the American presidential communication of tweets as opposed to press briefings. Millennials communicate and comfortably receive information this way. Yet, course material and training are, for the most part, still delivered in conventional formats.

A New Generation of Analysts and Intelligence Analysis

The next generation of analysts has much more experience with information technology and is much more comfortable than its seniors with information technologies, networked environments, and parallel processing of large amounts of information. Based on their use of social media platforms, millennials access data, share hypotheses, create "problem-centric" networks, and communicate in parallel with their friends in ways that will shape how analysis will be done in the future. Many experts feel the intelligence community will not attract, or will soon lose, these young people if it does not accommodate to how they think and learn (Glass 2017, Nevid 2011).

Therefore, how do we develop their classroom experience to take into account that the current and next generation of analysts are fast, not slow; do parallel processing, not serial processing; give pride of place to graphics, not text; do random accessing, not step-by-step processing; are connected, not stand-alone; are active, not passive; mix work and play; are impatient for results and very definitely see technology as a friend, not a foe? These characteristics can be the greatest future assets or considerable liabilities, depending on how these resources can be channeled.

Research results from a sampling of millennial students polled by Cynthia Phillips (2014) provided numerous proposals for engaging the millennial learner. Some of these suggestions included that professors do not read from PowerPoints because millennial students zoned out before the second slide. The results encouraged professors to do problems in class based on the reading material as well as explain how textbook and lecture material can be applied to the real world. Lectures longer than 15 minutes or that do not have other types of activities will not hold their attention or allow them to process and synthesize the information they are learning.

So, how do we teach them? Part of the solution might be multidisciplinary instruction that calls on millennials' strengths of collaboration and desire to work in teams for problem solving especially, their value of graphics and ability to find information online and create what they find into something new. This is also what is valued in an intelligence analyst. The Center for Educational Research and Teaching Innovation at the Missouri University of Science and Technology has an excellent resource for teaching millennials. It identifies the student issue, possible causes and teaching recommendations. For example, they identify the millennial issue of giving up too easily and lacking coping skills for failure, resulting from growing up by getting rewards too frequently. Have you heard of the participation trophy? They are also prone to quit when rewards disappear because they have been raised on extrinsic reinforcement. This gives them an unprepared mindset for success in college. Professors can mitigate this by providing specific praise for what needs reinforcement in the classroom like "persevering, trying again after failure, working hard ... give low stakes assessment throughout the course so students know where they stand. Help students understand how they learn" (The Center for Educational Research and Teaching Innovation 2014, see also Fowler et al. 2015, McCune 2017). This can seem completely mind blowing to a generation of professors who did not come of age (but might be raising) millennials.

Conclusion

Teachers, trainers, intelligence analyst managers, and program heads must begin to think differently about the millennial student and the future intelligence analyst if we want to prepare these students for educational and job success. Paradigm shifts have already occurred in the intelligence community and with the SOLs. It can be argued that the intelligence community overhaul post 9/11 was reactive but absolutely necessary as we moved into a world that was now preoccupied by non-state actors as opposed to the nation states of the Cold War. Higher education has had to adapt and adopt to information technology and learning platforms and there is speculation that by 2025 most college classes will be taught online. Like the Model T that seemed to usher in the modern age of industrialization, there are dramatic and constant changes that cause our world to shift. The millennial generation grew up without encountering a library's card catalogue, may have been in diapers on 9/11, and are the most globally interconnected students because of technology and social media. Higher education, if we want to prepare these students for careers as intelligence analysts, must take into account who the millennial generation is and what skill base and cognitive needs and challenges they bring to the table.

What is clear is that there are opportunities to refashion methods, enhance critical thinking, and reconfigure organizations for doing intelligence analysis and this can be applied to the development and shaping of coursework that will build upon the millennial generation's inherent strengths while providing a solid foundation in critical thinking. This does not mean we have to do away with lectures and reading, soft skill development, and honing excellent writing skills because millennials simply don't like doing it. What it *does* mean is that if intelligence education training is going to be effective and turn out competent analysts, it has to engage the millennial brain. How the intelligence education community resolves how course work is taught has to be overhauled just like the intelligence community had to be overhauled post 9/11. Just like we cannot approach the intelligence issues of the twenty-first century with tools from the Cold War, we cannot approach teaching millennials from a 1950s classroom.

Acknowledgements

Funding for this paper was provided by Syntelligent Analytic Solutions.

References

Brown, P. C., H. L. Roedriger, and M. A. McDaniel. 2014. *Make it Stick: The Science of Successful Learning*. Cambridge, MA: Belknap Press of Harvard University.

Educational Testing Service. 2017. *America's Skills Challenge: Millennials and the Future—Overview*. Princeton, NJ: Princeton University.

Fowler, D., M. Lazo, A. Turner, and J. Hohenstein. 2015. "Facilitating Program, Faculty, and Student Transformation." *Journal of Transformative Learning* 3 (71). 1-17.

Glass, C. 2017. *Sociocultural Contents for Teaching and Learning*. Lecture presented at Old Dominion University, Norfolk, VA.

Heuer, R. 1991. *Psychology of Intelligence Analysis*. Central Intelligence Agency.

Johnston, R. 2005. *Analytic Culture in the U.S Intelligence Community: An Ethnographic Study*. Washington, DC: Central Intelligence Agency Center For Intelligence Study, Print.

Kolb, D., et al. 2001. *Experiential Learning Theory: Previous Research and New Directions*. Case Western Reserve University.

Landon-Murray, M., and S. Coulthart. 2016. "Academic Intelligence Programs in the United States: Exploring the Training and Tradecraft Debate." *Global Security and Intelligence Studies* 2 (1): Fall. 1-19.

McCune, S. 2017. "Restructuring the Future." In *Creating the Future: Perspectives on Educational Change*. John Hopkins School of Education. Web, 20 Jan.

McGee, J. 2016. *Teaching Millennials*. University of Pittsburgh Medical School, University of Pittsburgh, May. Web, 10 Jan. 2017.

Neilson, L.B. 2010. *Teaching at Its Best: A Research-Based Resource for College Instructors*. San Francisco: Jossey-Bass.

Nevid, J. 2011. "Teaching Millennials." *The Observer*, May. Web, 21 Jan. 2017. Association for Psychology Science.

Oblinger, D. 2003. "Boomers, Gen-Xers, and Millennials: Understanding the New Students." EDUCAUSE Center for Applied Research.

Phillips, C. 2014. "Millennials and the Flipped Classroom." *Proceedings of ASABS*. Feb. 2014: n. pag. *ASABS Conference Las Vegas*. Web, 2 Feb. 2017.

Rainie, L., and K. Zickuhr. 2015. *Always on Connectivity*. Pew Research Center. August 25.

Reyes, S. 2016. "Military Weighs Mellower Marijuana Restrictions for Recruits." *CNN*, 02 Nov. Web, 10 Dec. 2016.

Rivera, B. 2006. *Millennials: Challenges and Implications to Higher Education*. University of Puerto Rico. 17 Nov. Web, 13 Dec. 2016.

Rue, P. 2002. "The Millennial Generation Comes to College." *University of Virginia* VI (2): Fall.

Schweitzer, L. 2010. "New Generation, Great Expectations: A Field Guide Study of the Millennial Generation." *Journal of Business and Psychology* 2 (2): 281-292.

Standard Center for Teaching and Learning. n.d. *Teaching the Millennial Generation*. Stanford University.

Stellar, J. 2017. *Education That Works: The Neuroscience of Building a More Effective Higher Education*. Ideapress Publishing.

Svinicki, M. D., and N. M. Dixon. 1987. "The Kolb Model Modified for Classroom Activities." *College Teaching* 35 (4): 141–146.

Tokuhama-Espinosa, T. 2014. *Making Classrooms Better: 50 Practical Applications of Mind, Brain, and Education Science*. New York, NY: W.W. Norton & Company, Inc.

Tapscott, D. 2010. *Growing Up Digital: The Rise of the Net Generation*. New York, NY: McGraw-Hill.

The Center for Educational Research and Teaching Innovation. 2014. *Teaching Millennials*. Missouri University of Science and Technology.

The Economist. 2017. "What's Next: Future Global Trends Affecting Your Organization." March 9.

The Next Great Generation. 2010. "Getting Gen Y's Attention." May 10.

United States Government. 2009. "A Tradecraft Primer: Structured Analytic Techniques for Improving Intelligence Analysis." March.

Weinbaum, C., G. Richard, and O. Jenny. 2016. *The Millennial Generation: Implications for the Intelligence and Policy Communities*. Rand Corporation.

Teaching the Intelligence Collection Disciplines: The Effectiveness of Experiential Learning as a Pedagogical Technique

Keith Cozine, Ph.D.[1]

ABSTRACT

Teaching intelligence collection within an academic setting can be difficult because of the clandestine nature of tradecraft and sources of intelligence. One course titled "Intelligence Planning, Collection and Processing," offered as part of the undergraduate Homeland Security program at St. John's University, requires students to engage in intelligence collection projects. Specifically, students are required to use techniques taught in class to plan, conduct, and process intelligence from open sources, human sources, and geospatial sources. At the end of each semester, data were gathered by a survey asking the students their perception of the utility of these projects in helping them develop a better understanding of the course material. Specific focus was placed on how the students felt these projects met the learning objectives of the course. Data were collected from students enrolled in this course over the span of three semesters, culminating in the Spring 2017 semester. This article presents and analyzes the results of these surveys in terms of how the students perceived the effectiveness of these intelligence collection projects in helping them better understand the class material and meet the course objectives. It is the hope that the research presented will not only shed light on the effectiveness of these projects but will also help guide the further development of experiential learning pedagogical techniques to enhance learning in both this course and other intelligence courses delivered in an academic setting.

Keywords: experiential learning, intelligence education, intelligence collection, intelligence training, tradecraft.

---

1   Keith Cozine, Ph.D., is Assistant Professor of Homeland Security in the Division of Criminal Justice, Legal Studies and Homeland Security at St. John's University. Dr. Cozine earned an M.A. in Criminal Justice and a Ph.D. in Global Affairs from Rutgers University where he also served as a Guest Lecturer. He has over a decade of law enforcement and intelligence experience with the U.S. Government. His areas of specialization include border security, international cooperation to combat transnational crime, and terrorism.

Resumen

Enseñar la recopilación de inteligencia dentro de un contexto académico puede ser difícil por la naturaleza clandestina del oficio y recursos de la inteligencia. Un curso que se llama "Planeación, recolección y procesamiento de inteligencia" que se ofrece como parte del programa de pregrado de Homeland Security de la Universidad de St. John requiere que los estudiantes se involucren en proyectos de recopilación de inteligencia. Específicamente, los estudiantes tienen que usar técnicas que se enseñan en clase para planear, manejar y procesar inteligencia de fuentes abiertas, fuentes humanas y fuentes geoespaciales. Al final de cada semestre, los datos recopilados por una encuesta que le preguntó a los estudiantes cuál era su percepción de la utilidad de estos proyectos en ayudarles a desarrollar una mejor comprensión del curso. Se le dio un enfoque específico a cómo los estudiantes sintieron que estos proyectos llegaban a los objetivos de aprendizaje del curso. Se recopilaron datos de estudiantes inscritos en esta clase a lo largo de tres semestres, culminando en el semestre de primavera de 2017. Este artículo presenta y analiza los resultados de estas encuestas en términos de cómo los estudiantes percibieron la efectividad de esos proyectos de recopilación de inteligencia al ayudarles a entender mejor el material didáctico y cumplir los objetivos de la clase. Es la esperanza que la investigación presentada no solo pondrá en evidencia la efectividad de estos proyectos, sino que también ayudará a guiar el desarrollo futuro de las técnicas pedagógicas de aprendizaje experiencial para mejorar el aprendizaje tanto en este curso, como en otros cursos de inteligencia que se dan en un contexto académico.

Palabras clave: *aprendizaje experiencial, educación de la inteligencia, recopilación de inteligencia, entrenamiento de inteligencia, oficio*

摘要

由于谍报技术本质和情报来源的隐蔽性，在学术背景下进行情报收集教学可能会比较困难。圣约翰大学（St. John's University）本科的国土安全课程中包含一项名为"情报规划、收集和处理"（Intelligence Planning, Collection and Processing）的课程，该课程要求学生参与情报收集项目。具体而言，学生被要求使用课堂上学到的技术来规划、实施和处理来自公开来源（open sources）、人力来源(human sources)和地理空间来源

(geospatial sources)的情报。每学期结束时，学校会通过一项调查来收集数据，这项调查将询问学生对使用情报项目帮助其更好地了解课程材料一事的看法。调查的具体重点则是，学生如何感受到这些项目达到了课程学习目标。调查收集到的数据源于到2017年春季学期为止的三学期里参加过这门课程的学生。本文分析了学生如何看待情报收集项目在帮助其更好地理解课堂材料、达到课程目标一事上的有效性，得出了调查结果。本文希望呈现的研究将不仅阐明这些项目的有效性，还能帮助引导对体验式学习这一教学技术更进一步的发展，从而提高学术背景下该课程和其他情报课程的学习。

关键词：体验式学习，情报教育，情报收集，情报训练，谍报技术

Introduction

The goal of higher education should not simply be imparting knowledge, but also giving students the tools and skills they need to be successful in their future career. This means utilizing pedagogical techniques beyond lectures and readings to give students hands-on, practical experience that allows them to apply what they have learned using more traditional education techniques. This hands-on approach to education is easier to provide to students in some academic disciplines, such as those requiring technical skills or the physical sciences where lab work is considered part of the regular course curriculum. Even in teaching the fine arts, it is often more about practicing and doing rather than simply reading and listening. The same is not necessarily true in the social sciences. While skills such as critical thinking, accessing and analyzing information, and communicating orally and in writing can be honed by assigning research projects, they do not necessarily mirror the type of work students will be doing in their careers. This is especially true for students seeking careers in the security and intelligence fields where operational security, concealing tradecraft, and source protection are paramount. This challenge is heightened when dealing with students within higher education or other students without appropriate security clearances. Those intelligence activities most relevant to the issues of the day usually come to light only if there are intelligence failures. One example is the case of weapons of mass destruction in Iraq and the reliance on an Iraqi source known as "Curveball," who fabricated information regarding mobile factories used to produce biological weapons. This is not to say there is no teaching value in investigating failure; however, focusing on successes allows a more balanced approach to examining the workings of the United States Intelligence Community (IC). Compounding the problem, when intelligence successes do come to light, it is often years or even decades later; this can be extremely problematic when trying to teach intelligence to undergraduate students who, in many cases, were not even in primary school on September 11, 2001 (Cozine 2015a). One way to bridge these gaps between the classroom and the real world is through experiential learning.

While critical thinking, accessing and analyzing information, and communicating orally and in writing are important skills for intelligence analysts, this is only one category of a career path within the intelligence field. For example, the Central Intelligence Agency lists Collection Management Officer, Directorate of Operations Language Officer, Operations Officer, Paramilitary Operations Officer/Specialized Skills Officer, Staff Operations Officer, and Targeting Officer as occupations within its Directorate of Operations (CIA 2017). The challenge is to determine how experiential learning can be employed to provide a foundation for the skills and tools needed in these occupations as well as instilling a better understanding of the concepts, issues, and challenges faced. One possible solution is to design experiential learning assignments and projects that are specifically focused on various intelligence collection disciplines. This is not to suggest that individuals in careers focused on intelligence collection do not need the ability to think critically, access and analyze information, and communicate both orally and in writing, as they clearly do. Likewise, students seeking careers as intelligence analysts can benefit from having a greater understanding of the skills and tools needed for intelligence collection, processing, and exploitations, and the concepts, issues, and challenges faced in delivering raw intelligence for analysis.

The purpose of this paper is two-fold—first, to explain how experiential learning is employed in the course *Intelligence Collection, Processing and Exploitation* as part of the curriculum of the undergraduate Homeland Security program at St. John's University in Queens, NY. During this course, students are required to complete three intelligence collection projects focusing on Open Source (OSINT), Human (HUMINT), and Geospatial (GEOINT) collection disciplines. The OSINT project requires students to collect raw data from the Internet in fulfillment of a specific collection requirement and disseminate it in the form of raw intelligence. The HUMINT project requires students to acquire a potential human source of intelligence that may have access to a specific type of information to fulfill an intelligence requirement. Finally, The GEOINT project requires collecting images of a specific target and processing and exploiting these images, so they can be utilized as part of a larger finished intelligence product.

The second purpose of this paper is to determine whether students enrolled in this course felt that these intelligence collection projects enhanced learning and an understanding of the course material. This was accomplished through the use of a survey of students enrolled in the course over several semesters in which they were asked about their experiences with the project. The data collected in this survey were analyzed to answer the research questions: (1) *Did the students perceive the experiential learning technique of requiring intelligence collection projects as part of the course requirements to enhance their understanding and comprehension of the course material? (2) Did it allow them allow them to apply this knowledge in a real world environment?*

Experiential Learning in Security and Intelligence Studies

Experiential learning is "Learning in which the learner is directly in touch with the realties being studied. It is contrasted with the learner who only reads about, talks about, or writes about these realities but never comes in contact with them as part of the learning process," (Kolb 2015, xviii). There are a variety of experiential learning programs offered at educational institutions such as internships, service learning, field projects, game play, and experiential learning projects that add a direct experience component to their traditional academic programs or course work (Kolb 2015). Some have argued that even utilizing television and film extend the learning beyond the textbook, such as helping students get a feel for an era or an event, interest building, presenting information in numerous ways to better help students understand topics, and providing teachable moments based on specific scenes or topics portrayed (Kelly 2017). Sprau (2001) believes that potential for instructional improvement in history using films within the framework of Kolb's experiential learning model is perhaps the greatest when instructors are faced with a wide array of students from majors with different learning strengths. These same techniques of experiential learning activities are being incorporated into course work and curricula in many security and intelligence studies programs.

Jackson (2011) described how he used game-based experiential learning in his course *Science and Technology of Terrorism and Counterterrorism*, offered at Georgetown University. In the game, the class is divided into two sides and plays against each other. One side acts as terrorists planning a short terrorist campaign against a hypothetical urban subway system and the other side is charged with protecting the subway system from attacks. A modified version of this game was also utilized in the course *Modern Political Terrorism*, at Rutgers University in Newark, NJ and *Terrorism and Emergency Management*, at St. John's University in Queens, NY. A study of students who participated in these experiential learning activities at Rutgers and St. John's found the activities deepened student engagement, increased the students' understanding of concepts, models, and theories related to the course material, and increased motivation and overall satisfaction with the course (Cozine 2015a).

Experiential-based learning activities are also utilized in intelligence-specific courses in academic and professional training environments. Game-based learning was incorporated into the initial training of the patrol officers responsible for protecting passengers, operations, and facilities at Aeroports de Montreal against all threats to civil aviation. The purpose of the activity was to demonstrate the importance and relevance of intelligence to their work and framed intelligence within an airport context (Palisson 2013). Wheaton (2011) explains how he incorporates this game-based approach to teach strategic intelligence analysis by utilizing online or downloadable games such as World of Warcraft. In addition to playing the games, students were required to come to some defensible conclusion about how the game related to the topic of that particular class. Experiential-based learning is used to teach intelligence collection as well, specifically the use of television and movies to teach about HUMINT collection. Cozine (2015b) describes how the television shows *Turn: Washington's Spies, The Assets,* and *The Americans,* and the movie, *Zero Dark Thirty,* can be utilized to teach a variety of covert sources of HUMINT including source acquisition, walk-ins, and agents working clandestinely in foreign countries, as well as overt methods such as interrogation of prisoners and detainees. It is not just game-play and film that have value as experiential learning techniques in teaching intelligence-related topics, but also experiential learning projects, specifically projects centered around intelligence collection.

Experiential Learning Projects and Intelligence Collection

Experiential learning projects are an important component of the course *Intelligence Collection, Processing and Exploitation* as part of the curriculum of the undergraduate Homeland Security program at St. John's University in Queens, NY. During the semester, students are required to complete three intelligence collection projects—one focusing on OSINT, a second focusing on HUMINT, and a third on GEOINT. The goals of these projects are: (1) to reinforce the course content presented in classroom lectures, the required text, and other course material; (2) to help the students achieve the overall course objectives; (3) to provide students with an understanding of the benefits and challenges of each collection discipline; and (4) to allow the students to utilize the knowledge and skills developed within the classroom to actually collect intelligence data and process it into raw intelligence within the context of specific intelligence requirements.

While each project was focused on a specific intelligence collection discipline, they also dealt with issues that crossed over multiple or all collection disciplines. For example, the TCPED process (tasking collection, processing, exploitation, and dissemination) is a process that each INT must go through, regardless of the source, in order to create raw intelligence that the analyst can use to create products to be used by policymakers (Lowenthal and Clark 2015). For this reason, the TCPED process is an important component of each project in addition to the discipline-specific content. In addition, many scholars agree that experiential learning does not teach anything by itself and some of the most important learning takes place in the form of a debriefing during which the outcomes of the activities are put into context (Palisson 2013). For all three projects, this debriefing takes place in the form of a classroom discussion where the students reflect on their experiences with the project and how it related to the course material and learning outcomes.

OSINT

Given that OSINT is often referred as the source of first resort, it would seem appropriate that it is the starting point for an exploration into intelligence collection. Within the course content, there are some specific characteristics of OSINT that need to be emphasized. First, information does not have to be secret to be valuable. Second, because it is not secret, there are a variety of sources where OSINT data can be acquired. These include: traditional mass media (e.g., television, radio, newspapers, and magazines), specialized journals, conference proceedings and think tank studies, photos, maps, commercial imagery products, and the Internet. The variety of sources also presents certain challenges, primarily the daunting nature of the sheer volume of data available. Separating wheat from chaff requires skill, knowledge, and a reliance on sophisticated information technology (CIA 2013). Third, is defining what OSINT actually is: information that is publically available, acquired through legal means that is subsequently vetted and analyzed in order to fulfill an intelligence requirement (Jardines 2015).

The OSINT project assigned is designed to provide the students with a better understanding of these aspects of OSINT, but also some issues and concepts that cross all collection disciplines. In this particular project, those issues are related to the issue of differentiating between intelligence requirements and collection requirements, and the applications of the TCPED process. For this project, each student was provided an overall intelligence requirement and a collection requirement concerning the data that needed to be acquired and turned into raw intelligence to help a hypothetical analyst fulfill a collection requirement. The students were given very little specific guidance on how to achieve this, as the goal was for them to draw from the knowledge and skills learned in class and the required readings. The project instructions were intentionally vague and simply stated:

> You have been provided an intelligence requirement and are tasked with a collection requirement or a request for information (RFI) for an analyst to fulfill the intelligence requirement provided by the consumer. Using any OSINT resources available, you must acquire (collect) raw data to help you fulfill your collection requirement. You will then process the raw data by putting it into a usable format. Next, you will exploit the raw data for validity, credibility, inherent biases, or any other information characteristics that may impact the

interpretation of the request for information. Finally, you will disseminate the raw intelligence by uploading it as a Word document on Blackboard.

The actual intelligence requirements and RFIs varied each semester depending on real-world events. For example, in the semester immediately following the November 2015 Paris attacks, one intelligence requirement given was: "In the wake of the attacks in Paris last year, what is the likelihood of a similar attack within the U.S. homeland?" The corresponding RFI was "a statement by ISIS regarding the United States potential targets and operatives within U.S. homeland." It is important to note that in some cases, students were given the same intelligence requirement but different RFIs to help fulfill this requirement.

Given the vagueness of the instructions, the variety of intelligence requirements and collection requirements, the different levels of comprehension of the course material, and the creativity of the students themselves, it did not come as any surprise that there was great disparity in both the quality of the raw intelligence received and the way it was presented. The actual projects submitted ranged from simply cutting and pasting entire articles found on the Internet to full-scale finished intelligence products that attempted to answer the intelligence requirement rather than just fulfill the RFI. The disparity in quality of the project was desired as the hope was that these projects would provide the material for the most important component of the project—the debriefing. A classroom discussion about the projects was the main focus of the class immediately following the submission of the projects. During this class, students were asked about their experiences with the project and how specifically it relates to the course content on OSINT. Students were then provided examples of other students' projects to constructively critique within the framework of the course content. The goal of this debriefing approach was to create an even deeper understanding of the issue, concepts benefits, and challenges of creating raw OSINT intelligence beyond the course material, lectures, and even the projects themselves.

HUMINT

Though HUMINT is often referred to as the source of last resort, it is the second collection discipline covered in the course. Since HUMINT involves any intelligence involving humans as a source, whether the information is provided in secret or not, both covert and overt human sources of intelligence are covered in detail in the course. However, some of the most important collection requirements for any intelligence service is to learn the plans and intentions of an adversary whether that target is a nation-state, commercial entity, terrorist group, or criminal organization. Achieving this often requires covert human collection by recruiting a well-placed human source who is willing to provide information on that target. The key to accomplishing this is the intelligence officer and his or her relationship with an agent or spy willing and able to obtain the desired secret information needed to fulfill collection requirements. It is not the intelligence officer him/herself that obtains the secret information, but rather that agent that he or she recruits that has access to the desired information and is willing to provide it (Althoff 2015). It is this process that is the subject of the HUMINT collection project.

Just as the TCPED process is utilized to go from collection requirements to disseminating raw intelligence, it is the recruiting or acquisition process that allows intelligence officers to recruit an agent and is made up of six steps: spotting, assessment, development, pitch, handling, and terminations. "Spotting" is where a case officer attempts to identify individuals with potential access to information of intelligence value. The "assessment" phase is where the officer tries to gain insights into the potential recruitment target by obtaining biographic information to verify the individual's identity and potentially assist in validating access to information of intelligence interest. If the initial assessment of the target appears positive, the officer will seek to move the target into the "development" phase in which ongoing contact is established to further build the relationship and gather more detailed assessment information. The aim is to develop a close, personal relationship that allows the potential recruitment target to more fully trust the officer. The "pitch" is the most critical phase in the recruitment process. It is during the pitch phase that the case officer "breaks cover" and reveals his or her true intelligence affiliation and asks the individual to work for them. If the recruitment target accepts a pitch, the operation moves into the "handling" phase. In this stage, the case officer formalizes the recruitment and "tradecraft" is introduced to ensure that the case officer and the agent can meet securely to avoid detection. The final phase is known as "termination" and, despite the sinister popular connotation, termination simply means that the secret "agreement" to provide protected information has been terminated (Althoff 2015). It is this acquisition or recruitment process that is subject of the HUMINT project of the course.

Students in the course will identify an individual on campus who is originally from a particular region of the world or has connections to that region. Each student is given a particular region such as sub-Saharan Africa, Southeast Asia, or Middle East, as opposed to specific countries, to allow for a greater pool of potential candidates from which to choose. Once they have identified a potential target, they will utilize elicitation and rapport-building techniques and the acquisition process to determine if their target or someone they know has access to information that may have intelligence value. To accomplish this, the students are provided the following scenario:

> After years of budget cuts, the intelligence agency you have worked for has a serious shortage of human assets in (assigned regions). You have been

tasked with recruiting individuals domestically who may be able to assist you in developing assets overseas. To accomplish this, you will need to do the following:

- **Spotting:** Identify potential asset. This should be someone born in this region of the world or with other significant connection to that region.

- **Assessing:** Determine the individual has access to someone overseas that may have intelligence value.

- **Development:** Determine the nature of that relationship and whether it can be exploited for possible assistance in recruitment.

- **Pitch:** Would the asset be willing to contact his connection overseas to gauge interest in possible recruitment? (**Hypothetically**)

- **Handling:** How are you going to stay in contact with one other to discuss progress and other issues that may arise?

After you have completed this assignment, you must prepare an intelligence collection report as to the results of your search. Remember, source protection is of paramount concern.

Again, like the OSINT project, how the students actually accomplish this and the format of the intelligence collection report is intentionally left vague in order to allow them to draw upon the knowledge and skills they learned in class to complete the project. The only additional guidance that the students are provided is that they cannot target anyone in the class, or someone they have a pre-existing relationship with, and once a potential target is identified, for safety reasons, the student must advise the target that this is part of a class project. Also like the OSINT project, the class participates in a debriefing session where they can discuss the different approaches, issues, and challenges they faced in completing the assignment.

While it is acknowledged that this HUMINT project is not a truly realistic representation of the acquisition process, especially when recruiting the most valuable agents can require months if not years, it is believed that the project has value as an important teaching tool. First, though it is not a true realistic representation of acquisition processes, it does introduce the students to the concepts behind the process and demonstrate some of the pitfalls and challenges of the process even at this basic level. Perhaps more importantly, it requires the students to interact with someone from another cultural background and shows the need for strong interpersonal skills in order to establish and maintain a relationship of this nature. These skills such as good communication, rapport building, and maintaining trust are important skills in all HUMINT collection whether overt or covert.

One of the interesting things to come out of the debriefing was the students who participated in class on a regular basis were also the students who seemed to have the most success with the project regardless of the region of the world they were assigned. There are clearly impediments to creating a realistic HUMINT collection project focused on agent acquisitions, but these challenges pale in comparison to developing an intelligence collection project focused on the technical collection disciplines of MASINT, SIGINT, or GEOINT.

GEOINT

Unfortunately, students do not have the resources of the National Reconnaissance Office or other technical collection platforms to collect MASINT, SIGINT, or GEOINT at their disposal. One way to offset this issue, at least in terms of collecting GEOINT, is Google Earth. While technically images acquired through Google Earth would be considered OSINT as they are both publically available and legally obtained, it remains a valuable tool in an experiential learning project to allow students to gain a better understanding of the various important issues and concepts from the course material related to GEOINT. These include: defining GEOINT as a combination of images, imagery intelligence, and geospatial information; the differences between absolute location and relative location; and the need to balance resolution, meaning how good the quality of an image is, and the need to see an extra bit of detail that is not there with synoptic coverage, meaning simultaneous coverage of a very large area of the earth to assure that important features are not left out (Murdock and Clark 2015). It also has value in demonstrating important concepts that impact all five collection disciplines, the need to incorporate use of all types of intelligence, or multiple-source intelligence (multi-INT), and the importance of the TCPED process in creating raw intelligence for analysis. The multi-INT approach is particularly important in GEOINT, because it is often other collection disciplines that provide the spatial data that is incorporated into the raw intelligence. The same is true of the TCPED process. A picture may be worth a thousand words, but only if the analyst knows what they are looking at. This means that the processing and exploitation of the images collected is crucial in creating raw GEOINT.

For the GEOINT project, the students are given the following scenario:

In recent weeks, ISIS released a video threatening to carry out similar attacks in the United States to those that took place in Paris in November 2015. The targets in the Paris attacks were dining and entertainment locations frequented by young middle class people. In response to this, the IC has been given the task of identifying potential targets in neighborhoods in various cities around the United States that share these characteristics.

To fulfill this intelligence requirement, the National Geospatial Intelligence Agency has been tasked with collecting satellite imagery of these neighborhoods and then processing and exploiting this data to identify potential targets, entry and exit routes, as well as assets that could be used in response to an attack. This could include police stations, firehouses, emergency services, hospitals, and any other assets that could be used in response to an attack.

Given that there already exists a significant database of satellite images of these locations in the DigitalGlobe library, the resources of the National Reconnaissance Office will not be needed. However, effectively processing and exploiting these images to create raw intelligence for analysis will require a **Multi-INT** approach. Important consideration should also be given to proper resolution and synoptic coverage when fulfilling this collection requirement.

Each student in the class is then tasked with a specific neighborhood within the United States in which they use Google Earth to collect images and then use OSINT to provide the spatial data and assist in the processing and exploitation of the images. Examples of collection targets provided to the students include Buckhead, Atlanta, GA; Coconut Grove, Miami, FL; and DuPont Circle, Washington, DC. Disney Springs was added to the list after it was learned that the Pulse Nightclub shooter, Omar Mateen, scouted that location as a possible target of his attack. As with the two previous intelligence projects, students were not given specific guidance on how to complete the assignment, again requiring them to draw on their course material. Also, this project has a debriefing element to point the exercise and individual assignment in the context of course material. The added benefit for this particular assignment was that the images that were collected, processed, and exploited by the students could be displayed to the course and students could brief the class on their particular target as well as discuss how their assignment incorporated the characteristics of GEOINT discussed in the course.

Evaluating Projects' Effectiveness

The hope of this experiential learning pedagogical approach of employing intelligence collection projects as part of the course's requirements was to enhance the students' comprehension of the course material; apply the skills and tools needed for intelligence collection, processing, and exploitation in a real-world situation; and provide a greater understanding of the concepts, issues, and challenges faced in delivering raw intelligence for analysis. Were these projects in fact effective in achieving these goals? Answering this question is challenging. One approach could be to have one group of students engage in the intelligence collection project and have another group of students serve as a control group that does not complete these assignments but only is presented with the course material through lectures and required readings. All the students could then be given the same assessment tool to measure their knowledge of the course material and the performance of the two groups as a whole could then be compared. The problem with this approach is that if the projects were successful in achieving their goal, only one of the two groups would have benefited from them. An alternative method is to ask the students who participated in the course how they perceived the effectiveness of the intelligence projects in achieving their goals. This was the approach that was taken to try and evaluate the effectiveness of these projects.

Methodology

The goal of this evaluation is simply to answer the research questions:

(1) *Did the students perceive the experiential learning technique of requiring intelligence collection projects as part of the course requirements to enhance their understanding and comprehension of the course material?* (2) *Did it allow them to apply this knowledge in a real-world environment?*

To answer these questions, data were collected from students who completed the three intelligence collection projects as part of the requirements for the course *Intelligence Planning, Collection and Processing* at St. John's University over a two-year period. Students enrolled in the course were asked to voluntarily complete a survey consisting of a combination of close-ended and open-ended questions related directly to their experiences with the intelligence collection projects. The questions focused on the students' perception of the projects' value as a teaching tool; specifically, did the projects enhance the students' comprehension of the course material; allow them to apply the skills and tools needed for intelligence collection, processing, and exploitation in a real-world situation; and provide a greater understanding the concepts, issues, and challenges faced in delivering raw intelligence for analysis?

The majority of the questions on the survey were close-ended or scale-type varieties, including attitude, importance, and rating scales. The reasoning for using these types of questions is for better organization and analysis of the data. However, recognizing the value of open-ended questions, some questions provided the opportunity to qualify the answers by providing additional information the survey participants felt was missed in the structured questions, or provide any other information or comments they deemed necessary. Using this type of question structure allows for the organizational benefit of structured close-ended questions while preserving the free flow of information and ideas characteristic of open-ended questions.

The survey consisted of three sections, with each section asking the students about their experience and perceived effectiveness of the project on their understanding of the course material as it relates to OSINT, HUMINT, and GEOINT. The first set of questions in each section asked the students to rank the impact of the particular assignment on issues or concepts about that discipline from "Large impact," "Somewhat of an impact," "Little impact," to "No impact." Next, the students were asked to rate how helpful they found this project in terms of the course material as it relates to the benefits and challenges of each collection discipline. The rankings for this questions were: "Extremely helpful," "Somewhat helpful," "Of little help," and "No help at all." Then, the students were asked the open-ended question of "The most important thing I learned or took away from this project was?" The final question of the survey was "Would you recommend that these projects be utilized in this course in the future?" The students completed the survey online via Questionpro.com, where the data were collected and stored.

Results

A total of 66 students enrolled in the course participated in the survey. As shown in Tables 1 through 3, with one exception, over 90% of the students responded that all three intelligence collection projects had a "high impact" or "somewhat of an impact" on their understanding of the course material as it related to each issue or concept that the specific project was targeting. In terms of the OSINT project specifically, as shown in Table 1, more than 50% of the respondents indicated that the project had a "high impact" on their understanding of each learning object with the exception of dissemination and the debriefing. Even in those two cases, just under 50% of respondents indicated that the project had a "high impact" on these objectives, 48% for each. The learning objective that received the largest percentage of students to indicate the project had a "high impact" was the collection phase of the TCPED process with 77.42%. When asked, "What impact did the OSINT project have on your overall understanding of the TCPED intelligence collection process," 75.81% indicated that the project had a high impact on their understanding of the overall objective of the OSINT project.

When students were asked how helpful they found this project in terms of the course material as it relates to the benefits and challenges of open source collection, 67.74% indicated that the assignment was "extremely helpful," 29.03% "somewhat helpful," and 3.23% "of little help." This means that 96.77% of students found the OSINT project at least somewhat helpful in their understanding of the course material as it relates to OSINT collection. The final question the students were asked was the open-ended question, "The most important thing I learned or took away from this project was?" As expected with open-ended questions, there was great variety in the answers provided. There were some key points that stood out as reoccurring in many of the students' answers. These include: how difficult it can be to sift through the massive amounts of information available on the

TABLE 1: *Experience and perceived effectiveness of the OSINT project on your understanding of the TCPED Process*

	Large Impact (%)	Somewhat of an Impact (%)	Little Impact (%)	No Impact (%)
What impact did the OSINT project have on your understanding of Tasking in terms of the TCPED process in terms of open source intelligence?	62.9	33.87	1.61	1.61
What impact did the OSINT project have on your understanding of Collection in terms of the TCPED process in terms of open source intelligence?	77.42	19.35	3.23	0
What impact did the OSINT project have on your understanding of Processing in terms of the TCPED process in terms of open source intelligence?	60.66	36.07	3.28	0
What impact did the OSINT project have on your understanding of Exlpoitation in terms of the TCPED process in terms of open source intelligence?	62.9	29.03	4.84	3.23
What impact did the OSINT project have on your understanding of Dissemination in terms of the TCPED process in terms of open source intelligence?	48.33	43.33	8.33	0
What impact did the OSINT project have on your overall understanding of the TCPED intelligence collection process?	75.81	20.97	1.61	1.61
What impact did the "de-briefing" following the OSINT project have on your understanding of open source collection?	48.39	45.16	4.84	1.61

TABLE 2: *Experience and perceived effectiveness of the OSINT project on your understanding of the agent acquisition process*

	Large Impact (%)	Somewhat of an Impact (%)	Little Impact (%)	No Impact (%)
What impact did the HUMINT project have on your understanding of Spotting in terms of the agent acquisition cycle?	59.32	35.59	3.39	1.69
What impact did the HUMINT project have on your understanding of Assessment in terms of the agent acquisition cycle?	65	30	5	0
What impact did the HUMINT project have on your understanding of Development in terms of the agent acquisition cycle?	61.67	33.33	3.33	1.67
What impact did the HUMINT project have on your understanding of the pitch in terms of the agent acquisition cycle?	64.41	32.2	1.69	1.69
What impact did the HUMINT project have on your understanding of handling in terms of the agent acquisition cycle?	61.67	30.51	5.08	3.39
What impact did the "de-briefing" following the HUMINT project have on your understanding of the acquisition cycle?	51.67	38.33	6.67	3.33

Internet; material does not need to be confidential or secret in nature in order for it to have significant value; the need to think outside the box to get the information you're looking for; and the need to vet sources for reliability and inherent biases. The issue of "fake news" was also raised by a number of students as an issue that made the project challenging.

As shown in Table 2, at least 50 percent of respondents felt that the HUMINT project had a "high impact" on their understanding of each phase of the agent acquisition cycle. The learning objective that received the largest percentage of students to indicate the project had a "high impact" was the pitch phase of the acquisition process with 64.61%. Once again, the de-briefing portion of the exercise received the lowest score with of 51.67%; however, still more than 50% of the students reported that the exercise had a "high impact" on their understanding of the acquisition cycle and an addition 38.33% reported that it had "somewhat of an impact."

As mentioned earlier, as part of the course content, students received instruction on communications skills, rapport and trust building, and how to elicit information in the context of collecting HUMINT. When students were asked, "How helpful did you find the classes on interviewing and eliciting information in completing this project?," 70% of the students responded that it was "extremely helpful" and 30% responded that it was "somewhat helpful." Not a single student responded it "was of little help" or "no help at all." This seems to indicate that communications and interviewing skills should be considered an important component of any intelligence collection course. To support this conclusion further, when students were asked the open-ended question about what was the most important thing they learned or took away from the HUMINT project, a recurring theme in the majority of the responses was the ability to observe and read people, the importance of having good communication skills, and the importance of building trust with a potential source.

The GEOINT project received high scores in terms of the project having a "high impact" on the students' level of understanding of the learning objectives of the project with the highest score for understanding the importance of processing and exploitation steps of the intelligence collection process in terms of creating raw Geospatial Intelligence at 75.93% and the lowest score for understanding of the concept of relative location versus absolute location in Geospatial Intelligence with a score of 68.52% (see Table 3). Conversely, the debriefing portion of the GEOINT project received the lowest scores of all the projects with just 42.49% of students indicating that this portion of the exercise had a high impact on their understanding of geospatial intelligence collection. Perhaps this is because of the technical nature of the discipline; actually doing the collection, processing, and exploitation is actually more important than talking about how you did it in terms of understanding the course content.

TABLE 3: *Experience and perceived effectiveness of the GEOINT project on your understanding of the course material on GEOINT*	Large Impact (%)	Somewhat of an Impact (%)	Little Impact (%)	No Impact (%)
What impact did the GEOINT project have on your understanding of the concept of resolution in Geospatial Intelligence?	72.22	24.07	3.7	0
What impact did the GEOINT project have on your understanding of the concept of Synoptic coverage in Geospatial Intelligence?	70.37	25.93	3.7	0
What impact did the GEOINT project have on your understanding of the concept of relative location versus absolute location in Geospatial Intelligence?	68.52	27.78	1.88	1.88
What impact did the GEOINT project have on your understanding of the concept of a multi-INT approach in processing Geospatial Intelligence data?	70.37	27.28	1.88	0
What impact did the GEOINT project have on your understanding of the importance of processing and exploitation steps of the intelligence collection process in terms of creating raw Geospatial Intelligence?	75.93	24.07	0	0
How helpful did you find this project in terms of the course material as it relates to your overall understanding of GEOINT?	74.07	25.93	0	0
What impact did the "de-briefing" following the GEOINT project have on your understanding of geospacial inelligence collection?	42.49	31.48	22.22	3.7

When asked how helpful they found the project on how the TCPED intelligence collection process is applied to creating raw geospatial intelligence, 64.81% of the students said it was "extremely helpful" and 33.33% said it was "somewhat helpful." This means that only 1.85% of students responded that the project was of little or no help to their understanding of how the TCPED intelligence collection process is applied to creating raw geospatial intelligence. When asked the open-ended question about what was the most important thing they learned or took away from the GEOINT project, the majority of the answers were about the need balance resolution with synoptic coverage or the importance of a multi-INT approach to GEOINT. It is interesting that these were not the areas that received the highest scores in the close-ended questions about specific learning objectives.

The students' responses to the questions about the value of each of the individual projects seem to suggest that the students see great value in these projects as a learning tool to teach about the various intelligence collection disciplines. It is perhaps the last question of the survey that gives the best indication of the value of using intelligence collection projects as a whole to build upon more traditional delivery methods of course content. The final question of the survey asked the students, "Would you recommend that these projects be utilized in this course in the future?" One hundred percent of the students responded yes.

Conclusion

The use of experiential learning as a teaching technique allows students to apply what they have learned using more traditional education techniques. Experiential learning has particular value in helping educators overcome challenges and hurdles faced when teaching topics related to intelligence, including the need to maintain operational security, concealing tradecraft, and source protection; students not having a security clearance to allow covering the most relevant topics; and relevant issues of the day coming to light only if there are intelligence failures. This last hurdle is particularly challenging when students do not have a firm grasp of history. This paper examined the specific technique of assigning experiential learning projects to teach intelligence collection, and how the students perceived the impact of these projects on their understanding of the course material.

During the course *Intelligence Collection, Processing and Exploitation* at St. John's University, students are required to complete three intelligence collection projects focusing on Open Source (OSINT), Human (HUMINT), and Geospatial (GEOINT) collection disciplines. The OSINT project requires students to collect raw data from the Internet in fulfillment of a specific collection requirement and disseminate it in the form of raw intelligence. The HUMINT projects require students to acquire a potential human source of intelligence that may have access to specific type of information required to fulfill an intelligence requirement. Finally, the GSOINT project requires students to collect images of a specific target and process and exploit these images, so that they can be utilized as part of a larger finished intelligence product. The goals of these projects are to: reinforce the course content presented in classroom lectures; help the students achieve the overall course objectives; provide students with an understanding of the benefits and challenges of each collection discipline; and allow the students to utilize the knowledge and skills developed within the classroom to actually collect intelligence data and process it into raw intelligence within the context of specific intelligence requirements. While each project was focused on a specific intelligence collection discipline, they also covered issues that crossed over multiple or all collection disciplines such as the TCPED process and the concept of multi-INT approach to create raw intelligence.

This paper also investigated whether these three intelligence products achieved their goal of enhancing student learning and understanding of the course material. Of 66 students enrolled in the course who participated in the survey, with one the exception, over 90% of the students responded that all three intelligence collection projects had a "high impact" or "somewhat of an impact" on their understanding of the course material as it related to each issue or concept that the specific project was targeting. The one surprising result was that debriefing portions of the exercises received lower scores than expected with only 48.4% for the OSINT project, 51.67% for the HUMINT project, and 42.49% of students for the GEOINT project feeling that the debriefings had a large impact on their understanding of that specific collection discipline. The reason this was surprising was that literature on experiential-based learning suggests that debriefing is the most important part of the exercise.

The intelligence collection projects appear to be an effective use of the concept of experiential-based learning to enhance the students' comprehension of the course material; allow them to apply the skills and tools needed for intelligence collection, processing, and exploitation in a real-world situation; and provide a greater understanding the concepts, issues, and challenges faced in delivering raw intelligence for analysis. That is not to say these projects do not have their weaknesses and could be improved. One major issue that remains unresolved is that these projects are only specifically designed for three of the five intelligence collection disciplines. The reason for this is that the author, because of the highly technical nature of these two other disciplines, has not yet been able to design projects specifically for SIGINT or MASINT collection. However, in terms of the other three collection disciplines, the students who participated in the three intelligence collection projects consider them a valuable tool. Perhaps nothing exhibits this more than the fact that 100% of the students surveyed recommend that these projects be utilized in this course in the future.

References

Althoff, Michael. 2015. "Human Intelligence." In *The Five Disciplines of Intelligence Collection*, edited by Mark M. Lowenthal and Robert M. Clark, 68-69. Washington, DC: Sage.

CIA (Central Intelligence Agency). 2013. "INTellingence: Open Source Intelligence." CIA. https://www.cia.gov/news-information/featured-story-archive/2010-featured-story-archive/open-source-intelligence.html

CIA (Central Intelligence Agency). 2017. "Careers & Internships: Directorate of Operations." CIA. https://www.cia.gov/careers/opportunities/clandestine

Cozine, Keith. 2015a. "Thinking Interestingly: The Use of Game Play to Enhance Learning and Facilitate Critical Thinking Within a Homeland Security Curriculum." *British Journal of Educational Studies* 63 (3): 367–385.

Cozine, Keith. 2015b. "Setauket to Abbottabad: The Value of Film and Television in Teaching Human Intelligence." *Journal of Strategic Security* 8 (5): 80–92.

Jackson, Brian A. 2011. "A Table-top Game to Teach Technological and Tactical Planning in a Graduate Terrorism and Counterterrorism Course." *Journal of Homeland Security and Emergency Management* 8 (2): 2–24.

Jardines, Eliot. 2015. "Open Source Intelligence." In *The Five Disciplines of Intelligence Collection*, edited by Mark M. Lowenthal and Robert M. Clark, 5–44. Thousand Oaks, CA: CQ Press.

Kelly, Melissa. 2017. "Pros and Cons of Using Movies in Class." *ThoughtCo.* https://www.thoughtco.com/pros-and-cons-movies-in-class-7762

Kolb, David A. 2015. *Experiential Learning: Experience as the Source of Learning and Development, 2nd ed.* Upper Saddle River, NJ: Pearson Education.

Lowenthal, Mark M., and Ronald M. Clark, eds. 2015. *The Five Disciplines of Intelligence Collection.* Thousand Oaks, CA: CQ Press.

Murdock, Darryl, and Ronald M. Clark. 2015. "Geospatial Intelligence." In *The Five Disciplines of Intelligence Collection*, edited by Mark. M. Lowenthal and Ronald M. Clark, 111–158. Thousand Oaks, CA: CQ Press.

Palisson, Arnaud. 2013. "A Board Game to Teach the Rudiments of Intelligence in an Airport Context." *Journal of Strategic Security* 6 (5): 281–297.

Sprau, Ryan. 2001. "I saw it in the Movies: Suggestions for Incorporating Film and Experiential Learning in the College History Survey Course." *College Student Journal* 35 (1): 101–113.

Wheaton, Kristan J. 2011. "Teaching Strategic Intelligence through Games." *International Journal of Intelligence and Counterintelligence* 24 (2): 367–382.

Peer Review Skill Development in Intelligence Education

John Andrews
Florida State University, Tallahassee, FL, USA

Dale Nute
Florida State University, Tallahassee, FL, USA

ABSTRACT

We identify three areas of pedagogical concern to aid in overcoming the challenges of acquiring information from multidisciplinary sources in geographically distributed locations and analyzing that information in a collaborative manner: developing the concept of an externalized analytical thought process among students trained via the lecture/rote memory model; developing the concept of sharing information, i.e., collaboration, among students trained via the individualist/competitive model; and developing the concept of formally critiquing the work of fellow students, i.e., peer review, among students trained that only the teacher has the answers. This paper focuses on the third concern while recognizing that all three must be addressed simultaneously. Conducting a peer review forces one to evaluate and thereby better understand the analytical process. Similarly, a peer review process can be constructed that forces substantive collaboration, even online. This paper presents the approach that we have taken to incorporate peer review at both the undergraduate and graduate level into the law enforcement intelligence curriculum at Florida State University.

Keywords: *Peer Review, Intelligence Education, Skill Development, Collaboration, Evaluation.*

RESUMEN

Identificamos tres áreas en la pedagogía que necesitan atención para ayudar a superar los retos de adquirir información de fuentes multidisciplinarias en ubicaciones geográficamente distribuidas y analizar la información de forma colectiva: desarrollar el concepto de un proceso cognitivo analítico externalizado en los estudiantes que están entrenados en el modelo de clase y aprendizaje de memoria; desarrollar el concepto de compartir información, i.e., colaboración entre los estudiantes entrenados con el modelo individualista/competitivo; y desarrollar el concepto de formalmente criticar el trabajo de los otros estudiantes, i.e., la revisión por pares, entre estudiantes a los que se les enseña que solo el profesor tiene las respuestas. Este documento se enfoca en la tercera preocupación al reconocer que las tres tienen que ser abordadas simultáneamente. Llevar a cabo una revisión por pares obliga a evaluar, y por ende a entender mejor el proceso analítico. Similarmente, un proceso de revisión por parejas se puede construir para fomentar una colaboración sustantiva, incluso en línea. Este documento presenta el método que hemos elegido para incorporar la revisión en parejas a nivel de pregrado y posgrado en el currículo de inteligencia policiaca en Florida State University.

Palabras Clave: Revisión por parejas, Educación de la inteligencia, Desarrollo de habilidades, colaboración, evaluación

摘要

本文识别了教育顾虑的三大区域，以帮助在不同地理位置克服从多学科来源中获取信息的挑战，同时以协作的方式分析该信息：（1）在经过课程/机械记忆模式训练的学生中发展"外部化分析思维过程"（externalized analytical thought process）的概念；（2）发展共享信息概念，即经过个人性/竞争性模式训练的学生协同合作；（3）发展正式批判同学作品的概念，即同行评审（Peer review），在该过程中，只有教师才知道学生相互批判的结果。本文在承认这三点顾虑必须同时解决的情况下，将焦点聚集在第三点上。实施同行评审时，一人必须给出评价，进而更好地理解分析过程。同样，同行评审也能以一种强迫"实质性协作"（substantive collaboration）的方式进行建构，甚至在网上也能完成这一过程。我们已采取措施将大学生和研究生阶段的同行评审一起整合到佛罗里达州大学（Florida State University）的执法情报课程中，本文对该措施进行了具体呈现。

关键词：同行评审，情报教育，技能发展，协作，评价

Introduction

"True genius resides in the capacity for evaluation of uncertain, hazardous, and conflicting information."

Winston Churchill

A good peer review may not be genius, but it does identify the uncertain, hazardous, and conflicting statements being made in an intelligence report. The intelligence discipline uses a variety of techniques to evaluate information. Peer review is a particularly important one, because it typically is used when someone expresses an opinion in a report and accuracy is crucial.

The idea of peer review/critique as a key action skill missing in many professional programs began with a sabbatical one of the authors took several years ago. He was recruited to work at FBIHQ as a subject matter expert in the Asset Evaluation Unit Counter Terrorism Section. It was at this time that the author observed a process where young analysts were required to conduct peer reviews of their colleagues' work products on a regular basis. These peer reviews were designed to improve the analytical skills of both the reviewer and reviewee as well as to produce an improved work product. After the year assignment was completed, the authors incorporated this technique in teaching intelligence courses. This was implemented not as an educational experiment, but to provide the students with the necessary skill sets to make them better analysts. Procedures for teaching intelligence students to conduct peer reviews in an academic setting were not published at that time, so we developed them to fit within the framework of activities already planned.

Describing peer review as an "action skill" characterizes our pedagogical philosophy that fundamentally, intelligence analysts are professionals, and by definition a professional is a practitioner. Therefore, doing something with one's knowledge should be as basic to an intelligence student as learning theoretical principles and working problems based on them is to a natural science or a math student. Otherwise, a student merely learns facts that rapidly become obsolete while a trainee blindly learns procedures that will soon be replaced by computer software. Neither scenario is satisfactory. We argue that universities and academies teaching intelligence must morph into the professional practitioner model currently followed by medicine, law, business, engineering, and most natural sciences.

Following the professional practitioner model, this paper first addresses the underlying principles and then the procedures employed to apply them. Finally, we comment on our observations using the procedures.

Principles

Aperceived need for increased numbers of intelligence analysts and for ways to reduce the initial training required for entry level analysts has driven the expansion of intelligence programs in the academic setting. Such expansion comes with the usual growing pains, the most basic being the curriculum. As usual with academia, the question of allocating time for both theory and practice within the time constrained academic structure spawns considerable controversy. The basic question, of course, is: what should a student know and be able to do upon graduation? After considerable deliberation, The International Association for Intelligence Education (IAFIE 2017) compromised by presenting one set of standards for education and another for training.

We feel this bifurcated approach begs the question. If the answer is "to analyze a problem," then the focus must be on "problem solving," not whether one is a technician or an analyst. We suggest that a generic problem solving methodology should govern the curriculum. Our suggested process is: receive the problem; determine what data is needed to solve the problem; collect the data needed; analyze the collected data; and report on the analysis. None of this is new. The steps may be expanded or condensed according to various authors, but these seem to be the fundamental methodology. What we feel is new is a protocol for assuring accuracy in the analysis rather than just "doing the analysis" and reporting one's results. On this note, Heuer, Pherson, and Beebe (2009, 68) in assessing the use of geographically distributed collaboration by analytic teams commented, "Many things change when the analytic thought process is externalized in a transparent manner so that it can be shared, built on, and easily critiqued by others." We believe that their observation about critiquing is not only true but critical to the concept of contemporary intelligence education.

For the educational arena, we identify three areas of pedagogical concern in the seminal statement of Heuer et al. (2009). The first is developing the concept of an externalized analytic thought process among students trained via the lecture/rote memory model. The second is developing the concept of sharing information, i.e., collaboration, among students trained via the individualist/competitive model. The third is developing the concept of formally critiquing the work of fellow students, i.e., peer review, among students trained that only the teacher has the answers. The convoluted nature of problem solving for intelligence dictates that all three concerns must be addressed simultaneously. This paper addresses the first two in order to provide context for the third concern, as it appears to be somewhat neglected in the education of intelligence students or at least it does not appear to have been published.

The education versus training dilemma is not new. The best known of the educational taxonomies addressing it was developed by Bloom and his co-authors in the 1950s (Bloom et al. 1956) While their taxonomy accommodated the technician and academic/paraprofessional educational levels, it was problematic for the professional level. By the 1980s, this problem had been identified to the extent that an entire issue of a professional educational journal was devoted to it. In one of the best papers, Carter (1985, 146) proposed a matrix taxonomy for professional education that is still unmatched to our knowledge. His matrix is reproduced as Table 1 below.

Table 1: A Taxonomy of Objectives for Professional Education

	Mental Characteristics:	Attitudes and Values:	Personality Characteristics:	Spiritual Qualities:	
PERSONAL QUALITIES	Openness Agility Imagination Creativity	Things Self People Groups Ideas	Integrity Initiative Industry Emotional resilience	Awareness Appreciation Response	**BEING**
SKILLS	**Mental Skills:** Organization Analysis Evaluation Synthesis	**Information Skills:** Acquisition Recording Remembering Communication	**Action Skills:** Manual Organizing Decision-making Problem-solving	**Social Skills:** Cooperation Leadership Negotiation and persuasion Interviewing	**DOING**
KNOWLEDGE	**Factual Knowledge:** Facts Procedures Principles Structures Concepts		**Experiential Knowledge:** Experience Internalization Generalization Abstraction		**KNOW-ING**
	COGNITIVE		**AFFECTIVE**		

Carter's matrix is an extremely powerful tool when constructing curricula in the intelligence profession. He identified three domains—personal qualities, skills, and knowledge—that are roughly similar to Bloom's domains of affective, psychomotor, and cognitive, respectively. Note that Carter is using some of the same terms as Bloom but he assigns them a different connotation.

The power of Carter's model comes when one recognizes that for each domain, there are two aspects—the acquisition (he termed cognitive) and the application (he termed affective). One acquires factual knowledge but only "knows" it through experience. Similarly, one acquires mental and information skills but one applies them through "doing" what Carter terms action skills and social skills. The personal qualities describe our mental characteristics, attitudes, and values, but these are really of importance when we demonstrate them (our being) via our personality characteristics and spiritual qualities. He uses the term spiritual in the sense of spirit, like in school spirit. In other words, Carter asserts through his matrix that a professional must have both theory and practice in their educational experience.

Carter's Taxonomy, in effect, serves as an excellent checklist when one develops a professional program. We believe, however, that Carter missed a key Action Skill—Peer Review—critical for the intelligence profession. Not only do intelligence professionals routinely practice peer review in the conduct of their work to ensure it is correct, but the process of conducting the critique reinforces their proficiency.

Application

Currently, an undergraduate degree and a graduate certificate in Law Enforcement Intelligence are being offered within the Public Safety and Security program at the Florida State University, Panama City. The undergraduate degree is offered both on campus and online while the graduate certificate is offered only online. Two courses in the undergraduate degree and one in the graduate certificate require peer review of projects or case studies. Our goal in both programs is to produce a student capable of providing an actionable intelligence product when faced with the uncertainty characteristic of a law enforcement situation. The peer review component is considered an essential part of accomplishing this goal.

We addressed the three concerns about teaching the analytic thought process—externalizing, sharing, and critiquing—by synchronizing them within a problem-based exercise. The exercise is usually a case study or project to simulate as much as possible a real-world scenario, thus achieving the action component of Carter's matrix. The analytic thought process must first be laid out in steps with examples of the content expected in each step (a report format and a rubric) before the students begin to construct a project. Collaboration procedures must be established, including groups with rotating roles that include a leader before the group can evaluate a report. And finally, the evaluation process must be established such that it requires substantive critiques and peer reviews that improve the initial product. This conceptual design was one of our objectives when constructing the programs.

In summary, the process we developed has five stages designed to synergistically develop the analytic thought process, collaboration, and peer review. These procedures are labeled as "Stages" in the following discussion of each concern.

Developing the Concept of an Externalized Analytic Thought Process

Areport is the traditional way to convey the results of an analysis; however, reports often do not provide the reader with the background used to arrive at those results. We constructed a report format that would allow us as instructors to evaluate the analytic thought process used by the student rather than just the findings. We labeled it "SitRep" as short for situation report. The principal purpose of the format is to guide the student to construct a transparent analytical thought process. A secondary purpose is to teach students to categorize their thoughts, to present them clearly, and to follow instructions rather than just write their thoughts and opinions.

The SitRep Memorandum is a combination of the military Situation Report and the civilian memo. The format was developed by the authors having only seven key elements and should never be over one-page, usually only one-half page (see Appendix D). The reason for the length restriction is that the Intelligence Community (IC) has found that policymakers operate under tight time restraint and seldom read over one-half page. The SitRep format acts as both a cover page and a conclusion/summary. It presents the administrivia, the reason the author is the one writing the memo, the problem that started it, and the executive summary itself. The key elements are backed up by a narrative and/or appendices, but the SitRep should be able to stand alone as an executive summary if need be.

The report for each case study/project uses the same SitRep format and the rubric associated with it. Thus, through consistent, frequent practice, the students become familiar with both the report format and the rubric for grading and/or evaluating it at the same time. More importantly, they become familiar with the evidence-based thought process.

Assignments typically involve research projects or case studies (see Stage 1 below). The introductory undergraduate course requires a project that walks them through an analysis of a law enforcement situation. That project is divided into parts to avoid overwhelming the students. Each part is graded by the instructor and then critiqued by the students. The second undergraduate course and the initial graduate course focus on using different analytical procedures for four case studies rather than projects. These assignments also are often broken down into parts both to avoid overwhelming the student and to allow more opportunity for the subsequent tasks of collaboration and critique (see Stage 2 below).

Stage 1: Research and/or Case Study Report—Each student will individually practice the aspects of a project or a case study that requires an analysis of evidence and a decision based on that analysis. These projects or case studies can amount to 40% of the student's grade and can take several weeks to complete. Each week the student submits a portion of the total assignment usually consisting of a structured analytical technique and value added analysis into a forum. These assignments provide the work product on which the students will conduct their critiques, collaboration, and peer review as described in the following stages.

Developing the Concept of Sharing Information, i.e., Collaboration

Students who study in a group usually do better than those who study alone, but studying together is not the same thing as collaboration. Developing collaborative exercises applicable for both on campus and online students is a significant challenge for instructors. Both learning them and administering them online is even more formidable.

As Nute and Andrews asserted in their paper (2013, 271):

> Professors who do require group work often give up. They find that students come in several varieties. Some students tend to control the group to ensure their own good grade. Some are slackers who ride on the dominant student's coattails learning very little and contributing less. The well-intentioned but less astute student who is completely baffled by the new requirement often just "goes with the flow" and contributes what the group requests but learns little of what the process is designed to teach. And, then there is the challenge of grading participation in a collaborative activity.

The logistics for collaboration are a significant problem. An intelligence problem requires planning, collection of data, analysis of the collected data, identifying gaps, recollecting, reanalysis, and reporting. All this can seldom be done in a single sitting whether face-to-face or online, thus multiple submission deadlines are assigned to ensure all the activities required are accomplished. Most of our students are working and/or have other commitments that limit their availability for simultaneous group work. Consequently, routine, individual assignments are submitted by a weekly deadline. These routine assignments are in the form of discussion boards or forums. They are in addition to the major projects or reports discussed above. There are also short exams given to the students to ensure they comprehend their reading assignments.

The discussion board assignments typically address a single issue. Stage 2 consists of group collaboration/critiquing these routine assignments. Because of the previously described challenges, the student requires extensive practice, which these weekly collaboration exercises provide. The students begin to develop their ability to critique their fellow students' work product in a constructive manner, which they find extremely helpful when utilizing the technique with more complicated problems contained in Stage 4.

Stage 2: Collaborative critique—Each week the student's work on the case study/research project (from Stage 1) is critiqued in a collaborative environment by fellow students in group discussion boards made up of four or five students, each one critiquing the others' work. The original response of each student is force moderated to ensure substantive original work which in turn leads to more productive collaboration. These critiques and group discussions help the student create a better work product. The main purpose, of course, is to develop the collaborative skill set for students traditionally trained to work individually and to compete with each other.

A second problem exists with collaborating on producing the project/case study report. Normally, an intelligence project may require the input of several skill sets (human surveillance, signal intelligence, and technical intelligence) to get the total picture of the project and often the data may be classified. In the typical class, neither the skill sets nor the data are available. Collaboration on a project thus becomes somewhat sterile, but it can still be productive. The procedure we use above in Stage 2 focuses on students providing help with the correctness and clarity of their fellow students' reports rather than assisting in producing the actual research product. This level of collaboration we term "critique" rather than "peer review."

Developing the Concept of Formally Critiquing the Work of Fellow Students, i.e., Peer Review

The peer review is a key task of the professional. Investigators, analysts, and scientists regularly review the work of their partners in a case. In the case of reports by the IC, such as a National Intelligence Estimate, they are always peer reviewed. On the one hand, if we take the time and effort to evaluate something, we are saying that it is important. On the other hand, if it really is important, we had better check it before signing off on it. One of the best ways to check it is to have someone else do it, thus the importance of peer review as a skill set.

As Nute and Andrews further asserted in their paper (2013, 271):

Evaluation is a fundamental form of critical thinking. It also is one of the most difficult tasks we perform. There are no set, computerized analytical techniques to rely on and most of our formal schooling teaches the wrong approach anyway—evaluation of the "answer" rather than of the process. In addition, with our society's emphasis on "getting along" and "self-esteem," students may experience emotional problems associated with reviewing the work of one's peers.

Basically, evaluation is a form of measurement. We are measuring the accuracy and clarity of something. If we are submitting an intelligence report, we want to know that it is suitable for action. But, we all realize that it is hard to proof read what we have written ourselves. We have all turned to a friend or fellow student and asked them to evaluate our work. A formal request for evaluation, we call a peer review.

Not only is evaluation an important intelligence skill set, but also it is a little used fundamental process for learning. Both of us have had extensive experience training professional practitioners. We both found that conducting an evaluation is an exceptionally good way to clarify thinking, both your own and the person you are evaluating. But, it may be the hardest learning technique to master. It certainly is the most traumatic. None of us like to be evaluated much less criticized, which most folk confuse with evaluation. But we both have found the benefits of doing it well more than outweigh the cost.

Upon our review of the literature, we found that other educators reported similar motivations for constructing peer review components in their curricula. Peterson (1973) opined that the benefit of improving patient care outweighed the cost of teaching medical doctors how to conduct a peer review and to accept one on their work. Lightfoot (1998) and Guilford (2001) both felt that the path to better scientific writing for their engineering students lay in learning the procedures of conducting a peer review.

Why is it so good? Knowing you are going to evaluate someone forces you to pay more attention to what they are saying/writing, and likewise, knowing you are going to be evaluated forces you to pay more attention to what you are saying/writing. Part of that attention focuses on the yardstick you are going to use to evaluate them. That focus forces you to figure out what both of you should be learning before the report is actually written. And, perhaps most importantly, the action of formally making the comparison between what your subject is doing and what he/she should be doing develops a critical thinking skill seldom learned anywhere else.

From an intelligence education perspective, teaching evaluation is a process perhaps as difficult as learning the process of evaluation itself. The steps we are presenting outline the process we are using. As indicated above, we distinguish between critiques in the discussion board system that informally help a fellow student create a more professional report and peer reviews that formally evaluate a submitted report more critically. In the report of the case study/project, a detailed rubric is customized for each report. Thus, the students can follow these rubrics somewhat as checklists to guide their collaboration and critique in the forums. Peer reviews, on the other hand, are intended to evaluate the report for its value as actionable intelligence using more in-depth questioning of the report. See Appendix A for examples of all three rubrics.

We use a two-stage process to develop the concept of formally evaluating the work of a fellow student. The first requires the student to think about the report like an instructor, which in some respects mimics the perspective of a supervisor. Since the peer review is graded, it forces the student to "take the gloves off" and engage the assignment. The second requires the student to collaborate with a group to not only share his/her ideas, but also to build upon them to create an even better report.

Stage 3: Non-Collaborative (individual) Peer Review—Each student completes a final report summarizing the previous three weeks of work that consists of an executive summary (SitRep), an in-depth narrative, and appendices. This is an individual and not a collaborative assignment. The instructor then assigns each student to a group and provides each group member with a report to peer review. This report will be from one of the students of the group who is assigned the role of group leader. Each student in that group, with the exception of the group leader, is to critique and grade the report utilizing the same rubric the instructor uses. This peer review is submitted only to the instructor and not viewed by any other students. This requires each student to study the report from the perspective of the instructor and not the student.

Stage 4: Collaborative Peer Review—The group will then meet face-to-face or online and the group members, in a collaborative process, will collectively evaluate the group leader's report utilizing their completed rubric from Stage 3 above. The intent in this stage is to provide cogent comments, questions, and examples with the goal of improving the substance of the group leader's report. The group leader will then prepare a final revised report based on the peer review of his/her fellow group members.

Stage 5: Feedback Exemplar Report—After the group leader submits a revised report, an example of an exceptional work product is provided for each student to compare to his/her work. This exemplar is intended to serve as a benchmark for their future efforts. The exemplars, as well as all papers, are stored in a plagiarism detection database so they do not show up in future years.

These three stages are obviously designed to provide evaluation practice from three different perspectives. This not only contributes to the student's skill set but also reinforces the concept that peer review is not a punitive action or a betrayal of someone, but rather a contribution to improving a work product.

Peer Review Purposes and Procedures

The peer review is written as if the student were a subject matter expert reviewing a report that was written by another expert on the same subject matter. The rubric for grading the report is given to the student prior to the peer review. The following excerpts outline the general procedures expected of students at different levels of experience with the concept of evaluation. The description of these levels and the criteria for grading as given to the student are presented in Appendix B. The mentions of types of questions refer to examples provided to the students to introduce them to the "science" of questioning. Students are also given a set of guidelines for the "art" of questioning, i.e., being tactful in the heat of the moment. Both lists are in Appendix C.

The three levels correspond roughly to the stages of the development of the student for evaluating a work product. As students get more experience with the subject matter and with peer review, they are expected to attempt the higher levels and to become more proficient. In the introductory undergraduate course, the first two levels are expected by the end of the semester while all three levels are expected of graduate students.

The first level is **COMMENT**: This level is a combination of proofreading for proper grammar and ensuring understanding of what the author is trying to say.

The second level is **CORRECT**: This level focuses on the subject matter and ensuring that everything presented is correct, e.g., facts are accurate, assumptions are appropriate, and the two are logically related to draw the implications or inferences asserted.

The third level is **COLLABORATE**: This level is the full-blown peer review. The student(s) collaborate with the author to fill subject matter gaps, to think of theories not thought of, to consider implications contrarily, and to offer alternate inferences. Not only are they to provide a different perspective, they are to ask the questions that challenge the author's findings and also promote new findings. These questions focus on cause and effect inferences, compare and contrast of similar events, benefits/burdens of an idea, structure/function of a proposition, perspectives of the participants, and considerations of counterexamples or different situations.

For each case study/project, at least one assignment requires a formal peer review "report." Students use a memorandum style report that includes the following sections: "What you understood," "What you perceived," and "What your questioned." The sections follow the three levels of evaluation described above.

Findings

As previously indicated in the Introduction, the authors did this not as an educational experiment, but rather to provide the students with the necessary skill sets to make them better analysts. No methodology was developed to track the students' peer review performance or to quantify their feedback to the technique. We did discuss the results of the peer review and attempted to fine tune the process for each subsequent course. However, there are a number of findings that, although anecdotal, indicate the benefits of utilizing peer review.

Less than 10% of students provide comments on their course evaluations and most of those include the usual complaints that there was too much work and too many assignments. Favorable comments indicated that case studies were preferred and particularly the feedback provided by the peer reviews, although one student complained that there were too many peer reviews. Other students observed that the groups had too few students in them, causing a problem if one of the students did not submit their critique. We, as instructors, however, were quite pleased with the performance of the students and therefore not only continued, but expanded, the peer review tasks as part of the curriculum.

Students initially balk at all three tasks—externalized analytic thought process, collaboration, and peer review. They do not want to follow procedures, especially if they are lengthy or if formats deviate from what they have learned elsewhere. They do not want to work in groups, especially with regard to sharing information for which someone else may receive credit. And initially, they do not want to critique other students, whether from a fear of not knowing how or a fear of retaliation of some sort, or both. That is to be expected. How do they change based on the procedures used in the exercises developed?

We overcome their resistance through the utilization of numerous evaluations to include peer reviews and critiques by the students. In one of our upper level intelligence courses, the student is evaluated 27 times during the semester to include 12 peer review assignments.

Obviously, this integrated approach to the analytic thought process, collaboration, and peer review requires intense participation by the instructor. All students are graded weekly on their forums and on their initial report. The group leader is graded on his/her revised report and the group members are graded on their collaboration and initial peer review. The role of group leader rotates with each report or project so students soon learn evaluation is not to be a personal attack.

Grading collaborative work is a lot of work for the instructor which makes it quite expensive for the administration but, as the saying goes, ignorance is even more expensive. We have been teaching intelligence classes using peer review of assignments for over four years. One of our major findings confirms our preconception that peer review is an important educational tool in the concept of learning by doing. The students have a completely different perspective when they assume the role of the instructor and that eventually translates to improvement in their own work product.

In hindsight, we reviewed what scholarly articles were available to see if other approaches might improve our structure, particularly reducing the amount of work involved for the instructor. We found no articles on teaching peer review for intelligence education, but did find a seminal article focusing on teaching medical staff to conduct peer reviews (Peterson 1973) and two articles discussing procedures for teaching bioengineering students how to publish and critique journal articles (Lightfoot 1998, Guilford 2001). The findings of the researchers for the three articles roughly paralleled our results.

Our peer review process was quite similar to that constructed by Guilford (2001), although he focused on reviewing journal articles. He also achieved a key goal of students learning to write in a style and according to guidelines that have practical relevance to their careers. Several of our graduates have commented that our report format is similar to that in their job. Guilford (2001) also reported that his students did markedly better on the major assignment when the peer review process was used than when it was not. We also observed a higher level of performance.

During the course of the semester, students became more proficient with the techniques and their critiques more specific. At the start of the semester, the critiques were limited to "great post" or "could have provided more data." They were very general in nature and not helpful. Since the critiques and peer reviews were graded with feedback, the students who received poor grades began following the rubric and providing detailed evaluations of their fellow students. For the face-to-face students, they were placed in break out groups and their discussions monitored by roving faculty. As with the online students, grades were assigned each week with feedback. Those students who spent more time with their smart phone than participating in discussions received grades that were reflective of this behavior.

However, we did have an unexpected consequence. When the students grade a group leader, they are grading the same assignment that they had just completed themselves. Interestingly, similar mistakes they made in their initial submission, which were not corrected when conducting their own proof reading, they found when critiquing the submission of their group leader. Consistently, over the four-year period, the students received a higher grade for their peer review than they did for their initial submission. A review of undergraduate and graduate courses show higher grades for the peer review exercise within a range of 10%–80%. This would appear to confirm the belief that it is harder to see one's own mistakes than to see mistakes of another.

One other observation is worth noting. In a majority of cases, the student grader was very critical in their grading and often gave very low grades. However, this tended to be more prevalent when their peer review was an individual assigent rather than a collaborative effort.

References

Bloom, Benjamin S., Max D. Engelhart, Edward J. Furst, Walker H. Hill, and David R. Krathwohl, eds. 1956. *Taxonomy of Educational Objectives: The Classification of Educational Goals, Handbook 1: Cognitive Domain.* New York: David McKay Co.

Carter, Richard. 1985. "A Taxonomy of Objectives for Professional Education." *Studies in Higher Education* 10 (2): 135–149.

Guilford, William H. 2001. "Teaching Peer Review and the Process of Scientific Writing." *American Journal of Physiology, Advances in Physiology Education* 25 (3): 167–175.

Heuer, Richards J. Jr., Randolph H. Pherson, and Sarah Miller Beebe. 2009. "Analytic Teams, Social Networks, and Collaborative Behavior." *Collaboration in the National Security Arena: Myths and Reality – What Science and Experience Can Contribute to its Success.* Topical Strategic Multi-Layer Assessment (SMA) Multi-Agency/Multi-Disciplinary White Papers in Support of Counter-Terrorism and Counter-WMD.

IAFIE (International Association for Intelligence Education). 2017. "Intelligence Education Standards." Accessed 8 May 2017. http://www.iafie.org/?page=IntelEd.

Lightfoot, J. Timothy. 1998. "A Different Method of Teaching Peer Review Systems" *American Journal of Physiology, Advances in Physiology Education* 274: S57–S61.

Nute, H. Dale, and John Andrews. 2013. "The Method to our Madness: Learning by Doing in a Criminal Intelligence Course." *Journal of Strategic Security* 6 (3 Suppl.): 267–280.

Peterson, Peter. 1973. "Teaching Peer Review." *Journal of the American Medical Association* 224 (6): 884–885.

Appendix A: Rubrics

Report Grading Rubric

The Grading Rubric is in two parts —Presentation (50%) and Content (50%). The Presentation Rubric applies to each of the four parts and will be graded strictly since you have been doing these tasks since elementary school and because, if you do them well, you will probably also do well on the Content. The Content Rubric covers the actual subject material presented in the SitRep and the discussion sections of each part.

Failure to cite sources in the text of the project, especially for cut/paste, is plagiarism and will result in a failing grade. Allowing another student to copy your paper also will result in both of you receiving a failing grade.

The Intelligence Community requires a "squeaky clean" background which includes your performance in the University. Poor grades can be rehabilitated, dishonesty cannot.

Presentation Rubric

	MASTER	EXPERT	APPRENTICE	NOVICE
FORMAT 10%	Format is as specified.	Format is as specified.	Format has only minor deviation from as specified.	Major format deviation or a portion missing
COHESIVENESS 10%	Ties together information from all sources. Paper flows smoothly from one point to the next and from section to section.	Information from all sources generally tied together. Minor disjointedness among points or sections.	Information from all sources not tied together. Major disjointedness among points or sections.	Does not tie together information. Points are disjointed and sections present disparate topics.
LITERACY 5%	No spelling, sentence structure, grammar, punctuation, diction or citation style mistakes. Good word choices.	Minimal spelling, grammar, or punctuation mistakes. Word choice generally ok.	Noticeable spelling & grammar mistakes.	Unacceptable number of mechanical mistakes.
CITATIONS 5%	Citation style is consistent and correct with published style.	Citation style is used in both text and bibliography.	All citations in text are not in bibliography.	**(Failing to include any citations is plagiarism!)**
		Citation style is consistent and close to published style	Citation style is either inconsistent or incorrect.	
BIBLIOGRAPHY 10%	Bibliography complete and annotations are informative	Bibliography complete but poorly annotated	Bibliography but either puffed with unused entries or some missing	No bibliography
TABLES and MATRICES 10%	Complete with labels & no errors	Properly labeled with few errors	Missing data, several errors	Missing tables, incomplete

Content Rubric

If you have paid attention to the presentation rubric, you will probably do a good job on the content as well. The format is intended to lead you to a complete project and a well-thought out one. It, however, is up to you to do the research and analysis that goes into the format.

	MASTER	EXPERT	APPRENTICE	NOVICE
PROBLEM REFINEMENT 10%	The problem is clearly stated The scope is appropriate for the assignment.	The problem statement is not clearly defined or The scope is not well focused.	The problem statement is a little vague or The scope is too broad.	The problem statement is vague and The scope is too broad.
INFORMATION COLLECTED 10%	Important requirements are covered with triangulation	Adequate amount of coverage for all requirements	Cursory coverage of topics	Some requirement topics missing
EVALUATE SOURCES / EVIDENCE UTILITY 10%	Sources are appropriate for the type project and adequate to justify inferences. All sources utilized are current and authoritative unless acknowledged as otherwise.	Some sources &/or examples not appropriate or adequate to justify inferences. Some web sites or other sources used are not authoritative.	Several sources inadequate or inappropriate to justify inferences. All sources used are credible and current, if not authoritative.	General failure to support inferences with sources. Not all sources used are credible, &/or are not current.
ANALYSIS 10%	All points in all sections are adequately discussed Sources are elaborated Critical thinking is apparent.	Adequate points & sources but not well connected &/or presented. More quotations than elaborations Critical thinking not obvious.	Pertinent content omitted or content runs-on excessively. Descriptions & summaries only. Too much cloak & paste.	Discussions are cursory. Elaborations are missing. Basically cut & paste.
INTEGRATION OF KNOWLEDGE 10%	Course concepts are used to integrate information collected into original insights. Conclusions demonstrate analysis and synthesis of ideas and ability to draw inferences.	Some concepts are not well applied. Some conclusions are not supported by evidence &/or concepts.	Concepts and information are presented but not connected. Conclusions are poorly justified.	Information presented but not concepts so any conclusions drawn are unjustified

Discussion Board Rubric

Levels of Achievement

Criteria	Below Expectations	Basic	Proficient	Outstanding
Critical Thinking Weight 20.00%	0 to 60 % Rudimentary and superficial. No analysis or insight is displayed.	65 to 75 % Generally competent. Information is thin and commonplace.	80 to 85 % Substantial information. Thought, insight, and analysis has taken place.	90 to 100 % Rich in content and full of thought, insight, and analysis.
Connection to Topic Weight 20.00%	0 to 20 % No connections are made; off topic.	25 to 50 % Limited, if any connections; vague generalities.	55 to 80 % New ideas or connections lack depth and/or detail.	85 to 100 % Clear connections to previous or current to situations.
Unique, Unduplicable Weight 20.00%	0 to 20 % No new ideas; "I agree with..." statements.	25 to 50 % Few, if any new ideas or connections. Rehash or summarize other postings.	55 to 80 % New ideas or connections lack depth and/or detail.	85 to 100 % New ideas and new connections made with depth and detail.
Timeliness Weight 20.00%	0 to 60 % Few to no required postings.	65 to 75 % All to some required postings. Some at the last minute without allowing for response time.	80 to 85 % All required postings. Some not in time for others to read and respond.	90 to 100 % All required postings. Early in discussion. Throughout the discussion.
Grammar, Stylistics Weight 20.00%	0 to 20 % Obvious grammatical or stylistic errors. Makes understanding impossible.	25 to 50 % Obvious grammatical or stylistic errors. Errors interfere with content.	55 to 80 % Several grammatical or stylistic errors.	85 to 100 % Few grammatical or stylistic errors.

Checklist Rubric

STUDENT NAME / CRITERIA	RATING					GRADE TITLE / Moskalenko Report	
	Missing 0	Scant 3.00	Semi-Developed 3.75	Developed 4.25	Well Developed 5.00	TITLE	COMMENTS
SITREP- Executive summary of narrative.							
Background who requested report and why							
Problem Statement							
Facts							
Sources							
Conclusion-Identify most logical hypothesis for the poisoning							
Reasoning-List the analytical techniques you used to complete Appendix B							
Recommendations							
NARRATIVE- Same headings except for Background as SITREP but more details and explanations.							
Problem Statement							
Facts							
List sources and credibility							
Conclusion- Rank various hypotheses of poisoning							
Reasoning (describe the techniques used)							
Recommendations							

Bibliography								
Sources								
Credibility and relevance of sources								
Appendix B								
Brainstorming								
Starburst technique								
List top three hypotheses								
Structured Self-Critique of best hypothesis								
Premortem Analysis of best hypothesis								
Appendix C								
Evaluate structured analytical techniques you used.								
TOTAL								
GENERAL COMMENTS:								

APPENDIX B: PEER REVIEW PROCEDURES

We devised three levels of peer review as discussed in the following. Know which one you are supposed to be doing as the questions you ask of the author and yourself differ depending on the purpose. Note that three readings of the report are recommended, one for each purpose/level.

COMMENT: Essentially you are a proofreader. You read the report to make sure there are no mechanical errors and that the writing is clear. You are ensuring primarily that you understand what the author is saying but, at this level, are not trying to be a subject matter expert. At the end of your review, the author should know what was done well and what needs attention. In some situations, this level may constitute the first communication in an ongoing collaboration. This is the bare minimum acceptable of an undergraduate but considerably more is expected of a graduate student.

READ THE REPORT—Keep an open mind, reading the report this first time to get the big picture, i.e., what you believe the writer intended.

- **Read the text carefully** for grammatical and spelling errors. Note these comments, clinically not confrontationally in your peer review report.

- **Read the text carefully** for statements that apply directly, or indirectly, to the topic question and also those obviously not relevant. Use highlighters to mark these statements and make notes of your thoughts about them in the margins. These notes form the basis for your questions soliciting more information or clarification from the author. Use closed-ended questions for facts and open-ended questions for opinions.

- **Keep an open mind!** Obviously, you are framing your ideas during your reading but the ultimate purpose of a Peer Review is not just to challenge the ideas and presentation of the author but also to challenge your ideas and perhaps even change your mind. After all, if you can't change your mind, how do you know you still have one?

CORRECT: You are a subject matter expert and as such you are trying to ensure that everything presented is correct—facts are accurate, assumptions are appropriate, and the two are logically related to draw the implications or inferences asserted. Alternative theories and inferences may be missing but it is not your job at this level to find them. You are to ensure that what is there is both relevant and reliable even though there may be more out there. You will focus on questions for clarification of ideas and on requests for more evidence supporting the ideas and implications. You will want to question whether the implications and inferences are being expressed with the correct degree of probability. If well done, this level of work is considered excellent for undergraduates and acceptable for graduate students.

REREAD AND ANSWER—Answer the key questions as you read it for the second time. You will be deliberate in this step.

- **Look for questionable statements**, such as where the author is stating his views, arguing for them, or raising questions. Since no author has unlimited space in a report, things must be left out. Often those things make the connections between the author's points. You should use your marginal notes to make those connections for yourself.

- **Look for omissions**. Other times, the author leaves things out because they might contradict his/her opinions. Note your suspicions so you will remember them and can request evidence to affirm or refute them.

- **Challenge his/her facts.** Do they seem reasonable? Why would data be wrong?

COLLABORATE: You, in essence, are the author's partner. You are collaborating with him/her to fill subject matter gaps, to think of theories not thought of, to consider implications contrarily, to offer alternate inferences. Not only are you providing a different perspective, you are asking the questions that challenge the author's findings and also promote new findings. These questions focus on cause & effect inferences, compare and contrast of similar events, benefits/burdens of an idea, structure/function of a proposition, perspectives of the participants, and considerations of counterexamples or different situations. Well done, this level of work is considered excellent for graduate students.

REREAD AND ANSWER—Answer the key questions as you read it for the third time. You will be looking beyond the obvious in this step.

- **Challenge his/her ideas.** Are they relevant in real-life? Why or why not? Make connections between the ideas in the report and what you know from your own experience and that of others.

- **Challenge his/her opinions.** An inference is a logical connection between a new set of facts and the principles you already know. The author's inference can be wrong because the facts are wrong, because the principles are wrong, or because the principles do not logically apply to the facts in this case. If you can't challenge any of the three, you may have to challenge your own thinking.

Peer Review Report

For each case study/project, at least one assignment requires a formal peer review "report." These are the general instructions for that report.

WRITE YOUR RESPONSE—Use your observations and the answers to your questions by the author of the report to write up your peer review. Use a memo style that includes the following sections. Obviously, they follow the three levels of evaluation above.

> **What you understood**—Briefly summarize what you believe is the author's main point. That way if you are mistaken, it explains your comments in the following sections. Any questions then go towards clarity. Comments on grammar and format mistakes are included here.

> **What you perceived**—This is where you point out the strengths as well as the weaknesses of the report both mechanically and cognitively. You challenge the facts, assumptions, and logic that lead to the implications and inferences asserted.

> **What you questioned**—This is where you really benefit the author. These are the collaboration questions that challenge the facts, assumptions, and logic at the deeper levels. You are looking not just for mistakes committed but those of omission as well. Questions go to alternative inferences from the facts and competing theories.

Appendix C: Handouts for Students

The following questions and techniques have been collected over the years from a variety of sources. An attempt was made to determine their provenance to no avail. If you know the origin, please advise us and we will give due credit. jandrews@pc.fsu.edu

Evaluative Questions

The Peer Review, and other evaluation techniques, are used in a variety of disciplines and for a variety of purposes. A set of general, stock questions have been developed over the years that will help you get started. These questions can be considered the "science" of questioning. They will sound and feel artificial for awhile but will become natural with use. Most of the time you will want to pick and choose among them, not only to evaluate the thinking of the person you are reviewing but also to stimulate your own. Before addressing the questions, we remind ourselves of the two basic types of questions.

Two Types of Questions

Closed-Ended questions are useful to establish the facts everyone can agree on before tackling the open-ended discussion. Examples are Who-What-When-Where-How.

Open-Ended questions are normally preferred for actual learning since they stimulate discussion and exploration. Such questions often start with "Why do you think that ...? Such questions cannot be answered by yes-no or single word responses. Once you get someone talking, they usually have something to say.

Sample Questions and Response Formats

Now we look at the questions themselves and how they are used. Since evaluative questions are used for more purposes than just peer reviews of reports, we give a variety of examples. As you get more familiar with them, you will find yourself modifying them to fit the type of evaluation you are conducting.

The questions are organized into categories based on what you are trying to accomplish with them. Most are also phrased for conversation but they are easily adapted to written.

Solicit Questions

After reading the report, what are some things that you wonder about?

After researching that event, what more would you like to know about it?

After reviewing our discussion, are there unanswered question we should remember?

Clarification Requests

(Colleague's name), I am not familiar with the information/experience you are talking about. Could you tell me more?

(Colleague's name), I am not sure why you said (the colleague's idea). Could you reword your comments to help me understand?

(Colleague's name), I am not sure why you do not like my position of (your idea). Are you taking into account information different from what I have considered?

(Colleague's name), I am not sure why you do not like my position of (your idea). Do you see gaps in my reasoning I have missed?

(Colleague's name), I am not sure but I think you are saying (your paraphrase of the colleague's idea). Am I correct?

Sample Agreeing / Disagreeing Responses

I agree with (colleague's name) idea that (the colleague's idea) because (a fact or idea they presented), but I want to add another reason why I think his/her idea is true (another reason).

I disagree with (colleague's name) idea that (the colleague's idea) because (your fact that contradicts his/her idea)

(Colleague's name), I understand your point/idea, (the colleague's idea), but want to present another side (your idea) because of (your rationale).

I am not familiar with the information/experience related by (colleague's name). Has anyone had a similar (or different) information/experience?

Request for Evidence/Support Questions

That is an interesting thought, can you give us an example of how it would work?

I don't remember that statement. Where in the background material did you find it?

I did not run across the information in my research. Where did you find it?

That action certainly is an option. What would be a good reason for them to do that?

That is an important point. What evidence do we have that supports it?

Cause and Effect

Ok, we agree that (an event of importance) happened. Why do you think it happened?

How could (an event of importance) have been prevented?

Do you think that (an event of importance) would happen that way again? Why or why not?

What are some reasons why people react that way?

Compare / Contrast

How are (a point/event of importance) and (another point/event of interest) alike? How are they different?

What is similar to (a point/event of importance) ?

I have a bad feeling about that point. Any idea why I might feel differently about it than about (another point of interest)?

What does (a point/event of importance) remind you of?

Benefits / Burdens

What are some of the reasons why this would or would not be a good idea?

So far everyone has been in agreement. That's not a good sign. Would anyone like to speak to the opposite side?

Those are some reasons (an idea) would work; what are reasons it might not work?

Point of View / Perspective

That (an event of importance) was unusual. What do you think he/she was thinking?

That group might not like that idea, but can you think of someone who would?

(Colleague's name) has expressed a different opinion/idea. Are there other opinions? Does anyone have a different interpretation?

Structure / Function

If that (an implication for an event) was the goal, what do you think about us doing (an action / reaction)?

That was an odd thing to do. What were their choices in that situation and why might they not have realized it? What would have been better choices?

Why would they do that? What do you think of their approach?

Could this situation be better controlled by changing the rules, changing the rhetoric, or changing the environment?

Counterexample / Different Situation

That was a costly reaction to (an event of importance). Do you think that would still happen?

That was a costly reaction to (an event of importance). What might be different today?

That was a costly reaction to (an event of importance). What might be different from what has happened before?

If (an event of importance) were to happen here, it would be a disaster. Can you describe a situation that might make us less vulnerable?

Suppose (an event of importance) were to happen. Would your implication still be true? Why or why not?

Technique Guidelines

Finally, your peer review is to be constructive which usually requires civility, if not diplomacy. Getting cooperation in an investigation or evaluation often depends on the tact of the questioner. Asking probing questions without offending the person being questioned is an "art." The following guidelines will help you remember techniques that have proven helpful to those learning to evaluate the work of others.

Be constructive, not personal. Evaluate the writing not the writer. Your purpose as a peer reviewer is to assist the writer of the report. A "yes man" helps no one. You want to be honest but not harsh. You phrase your comments as questions and suggestions, not as commands. If the writer wants to ignore your critique, your insistence will not accomplish anything anyway.

Do not rewrite the report. Even if you are collaborating, and your opinion is different, be reasonable. You can always write a dissenting report if you feel the writer is wrong and your suggestions do not inspire him/her to revisit his/her opinions. If a concise peer review does not get the job done, a lengthy one certainly will not.

Think, don't memorize. Evaluation is not a memory test but rather a thinking exercise. Keep your notes and text handy. Refer to them as often as needed. Cite them in your answers or report.

Be specific. Words such as "interesting" "vague" and "unclear" are useless. Likewise, you "liking" it or "agreeing" with it generally is irrelevant. Don't say such platitudes! Overcoming this tendency appears to be the most difficult task for the student.

Be an active listener or reader. Paraphrasing or summarizing what you think your colleague meant is helpful to both of you as well as to the rest of the group.

Discuss the ideas of the report, not each other's opinions. Opinions are like belly buttons, everyone has one and they are relatively uninteresting. The only thing of interest about an opinion is the facts behind it. Give evidence and examples to support your responses.

Show respect for differing ideas, thoughts, and values. After all, when everything is said & done, they may have become yours. Keep your mind open to the new ideas and possibilities being presented by your colleagues. Always winning an argument but seldom being correct is a sure way to be the butt of your colleagues' humor.

Disagree respectfully. Respect does not mean agreeing. It means you have thought about your colleague's idea and you have a **reason** for agreeing or disagreeing. When you disagree, you are not challenging your colleague but rather explaining your position to the group, obviously including the evidence behind your opinion. Learning to disagree constructively is a challenge for some.

Give credit when credit is due. This is another form of respect towards your colleagues. If you are building upon one of their ideas, say so while explaining yours.

Ask for clarification when you do not understand a question or someone's answer. Don't be shy about this. A Peer Review is not meant to confuse but to clarify. Understanding the question and the facts are critical components of critical thinking. Sometimes you just have to ask for more information. Your colleague may see a relevant connection that is obvious only to him/her. That doesn't mean it is wrong, it means you may have to ask for help to see the relevance.

Ask for the evidence. One of the most important clarifications is to determine whether the statement in question is a fact or an assumption, a principle or a point of view, or an evidence-based inference (a set of facts logically connected to a principle). Basically our reasoning adds new facts to what we already "know" but we want to make sure whether it is a real fact or just an assumption on your part.

Practice explaining. The least effective method of learning is listening to a lecture. The most effective is when you teach someone else. Keep in mind that while you are trying to learn the material, you also are trying to explain what you know. Address your colleagues in your speaking/writing, not the leader/teacher. I will be monitoring and sometimes asking a question of my own but the success is your learning not my opinions.

Participate! Your mother may have told you that you don't learn anything with your mouth open but in this case that is not true. Your participation requires both asking and answering questions. Participation is the key factor in your grade. More importantly, the ability to write your thoughts helps to clarify them.

Don't worry if things get off to a slow start. You are learning several new skills, like listening to your fellow students instead of the teacher for answers and being helpful to them instead of trying to put them down to impress the teacher as to how smart you are. Also, groups take a while to gel, some longer than others. Part of your learning is how to get your group on task quickly and effectively. Don't dawdle, however.

Appendix D: The SitRep Format

MEMORANDUM

TO: Lawen Order, Sheriff
FROM: Your Name, Intelligence Analyst
SUBJECT: Gang Risk Analysis Study—Asset Assessment Section
DATE: 4 Nov 2017

---

1. **Background**—(*Why you are doing this*) **aka Reference.** Other than Lt. Fuzz, most folk do not volunteer without good reason. If you are writing this because the boss told you to, say so up front as he/she may have forgotten. If it is your idea, this is a place to concisely sell why you spent all this effort before the reader gets involved in the details. Ex: Based on the possible presence of a criminal gang moving into the County, the following analysis is presented per your request.

2. **Problem Statement**—(*What is the problem*) Present a clear, concise statement of what is needed and what you plan on doing (scope) in other words what is your assignment. Each of the four parts will have a different problem statement. This paragraph is critical. If nothing else, it somewhat covers you if you misunderstood the assignment. (Ignorance of the assignment is not an excuse in this class.)

3. **Facts**—(*What you know*) This paragraph should be no more than a couple of sentences that in effect "headline" the topic.

4. **Sources**—(*Why you know it*) This paragraph summarizes the evidence. Sources, such as newspaper articles, special intelligence, satellite imagery, etc., can be used followed by the information from each source. Summarize each source and possibly its credibility.

5. **Conclusion**—(*What you think it means*) This paragraph provides your inference and possibly the level of uncertainty. This paragraph is basically the results of your work in other words your conclusion. Based on your research does this group represent a credible threat. Again this paragraph is no more than a couple sentences. Policy-makers have a lot on their minds and are easily confused. Keep it simple!

6. **Reasoning**—(*Why you think that*) This paragraph provides your reasoning for coming up with your results or consequences. How did you come up with your results. Describe the research you conducted.

7. **Recommendations**—(*What you think should be done*) There is considerable disagreement about whether an analyst should make recommendations to a decision-maker. Our position for this class is that the purpose of an analyst or intelligence officer is to produce "actionable intelligence." In future courses, this will be a ranking of courses of action (CoA) with an analysis of the certainty involved for each but for now, you are just giving the Sheriff an option or two about what else needs to be done.

Teaching Intelligence Analysis:
An Academic and Practitioner Discussion

Richard J. Kilroy, Jr.
Assistant Professor, Politics, Coastal Carolina University
Conway, South Carolina, USA

ABSTRACT

For many years, there has been an ongoing debate over intelligence analysis: is it an art or science?; tradecraft or training?; creative or critical thinking? As a result, academics and practitioners often differ in their views of how to teach intelligence analysis. On May 23, 2017, at this year's International Associate for Intelligence Education (IAFIE) Conference in Charles Town, West Virginia, a roundtable composed of faculty members from five universities in the United States shared their views on how they approach the teaching of intelligence analysis within their specific academic departments and disciplines. These include graduate and undergraduate degree programs; intelligence-specific majors or minors; multidisciplinary programs; traditional liberal arts programs; and professional school programs. They also come from diverse backgrounds as academics, scholars, practitioners, or all of the above. This article summarizes the views shared by the roundtable participants regarding how they approach teaching intelligence analysis, to include pedagogy; methodology; learning outcomes; assessment methods; course content; use of analytical tools and structured analytical techniques; and simulations and exercises.

Keywords: Intelligence, Analysis, Pedagogy, Methodology, Teaching

RESUMEN

Por muchos años ha habido un debate acerca del análisis de inteligencia: ¿Es un arte o es ciencia?; ¿oficio o entrenamiento?; ¿pensamiento creativo o pensamiento crítico? Como resultado, los académicos y los profesionales a menudo difieren en su visión de cómo enseñar el análisis de inteligencia. El 23 de mayo de 2017, en la conferencia de International Associate for Intelligence Education (IAFIE) en Charles Town, Virginia Occidental, una mesa redonda compuesta de diferentes miembros de cinco universidades en los Estados Unidos compartieron sus puntos de vista acerca de los métodos con que se enseña el análisis de inteligencia dentro de sus departamentos y disciplinas específicos. Estos incluyen programas de pregrado y posgrado; especializaciones académicas en inteligencia; programas multidisciplinarios; programas tradicionales de *Liberal Arts*; y programas de escuela profesional. También provienen de diferentes disciplinas como académicos, investigadores, profesionales o todo lo ya mencionado. Este artículo resume los puntos de vista que comparten todos los participantes de la mesa redonda en relación con la enseñanza del análisis de inteligencia, para incluir la pedagogía; metodología; resultados del aprendizaje; métodos de evaluación; contenido del curso; uso de herramientas analíticas y técnicas analíticas estructurales; y simulacros y ejercicios.

Palabras clave: *inteligencia, análisis, pedagogía, metodología, enseñanza*

摘要

多年来，关于情报分析的辩论一直都在进行：情报分析是一种艺术还是科学？是谍报技术还是训练？是创新性思维还是批判性思维？辩论结果则是，大学教师和从业人员时常在如何进行情报分析教学一事上持有不同观点。2017年5月23日，美国西弗吉尼亚查尔斯镇举办了国际情报教育协会（International Associate for Intelligence Education，简称IAFIE）会议，该圆桌会议由5所大学的教师参加，他们分享了各自如何在其特定的学术部门和学科下进行情报分析教学。分享的观点包括研究生和本科生学位课程、以情报为主修或辅修的课程、跨学科课程、传统自由艺术课程、以及专业学校课程。与会人员同时也是来自不同背景的大学教师、学者和从业人员。本文对圆桌会议参与者关于如何进行情报分析教学分享的观点进行了总结，从而将教学法、方法论、学习成果、评估方法、课程内容、分析工具的使用、结构化分析技术（structured analytical techniques）的使用、模拟法以及练习包括在内。

关键词：情报，分析，教学法，方法论，教学

Introduction

> Tale as old as time
>
> Tune as old as song
>
> Bitter sweet and strange
>
> Finding you can change
>
> Learning you were wrong
>
> (Ashman and Menken 1991)

This may be a song lyric from a Disney movie, but it could also be an appropriate description of how academics and practitioners often differ in their views of intelligence analysis: Art or science? Tradecraft or training? Creative or critical thinking? Beauty or beast?

On May 23, 2017, at this year's International Association for Intelligence Education (IAFIE) Conference in Charles Town, WV, a roundtable composed of faculty members from five universities in the United States shared their views on how they approach the teaching of intelligence analysis within their specific academic departments and disciplines. These include graduate and undergraduate degree programs; intelligence-specific majors or minors; multidisciplinary programs; traditional liberal arts programs; and professional school programs. They also come from diverse backgrounds as academics, scholars, practitioners, or all of the above.

Roundtable Participants

Dr. Stephen Coulthart, Assistant Professor of National Security Studies at the University of Texas, El Paso (UTEP), teaches intelligence analysis courses in support of two degree programs: a Master of Science in Intelligence and National Security and a Minor in Intelligence and National Security. UTEP's graduate program is certified by the International Association for Intelligence Education. UTEP also offers an open source certificate, the first in the country that offers curriculum not found in many civilian institutions, such as: social media intelligence; commercial imagery; and geospatial intelligence. At the undergraduate level UTEP offers an online Bachelor of Arts in Security Studies.

Dr. Stephen Marrin, Associate Professor of Intelligence Analysis at James Madison University (JMU) in Harrisonburg, VA, is the Program Director for the undergraduate Bachelor of Science in Intelligence Analysis (IA) degree program. It is administered as part of the multidisciplinary Department of Integrated Science and Technology (ISAT). The JMU Intelligence Analysis program is undergraduate only, with about 250 students in the major. There are two primary concentrations: national security and competitive intelligence, with law enforcement possible if the students minor in criminal justice. JMU's technical specialties include cyber intelligence (linked to computer science), and geospatial intelligence (linked to geographic sciences). It may be best to think of JMU's program more as an "analysis" major, which sets its graduates up well for a wide variety of different kinds of jobs to include—but not limited to—intelligence analysis.

Sarah Miller Beebe, Adjunct Faculty, Johns Hopkins University (JHU), teaches intelligence analysis courses in the Krieger School of Arts and Sciences, Advanced Academic Programs and Graduate Degree Programs at JHU's Washington, D.C. campus. The course is offered as part of the five-course Intelligence Certificate. The Certificate may also be combined with four graduate degree programs: Master of Arts in Global Studies; Master of Arts in Government; Master of Science in Government Analytics; or Master of Arts in Public Management. The majority of students who pursue the Certificate do so in the context of their Master's degree. JHU views this Intelligence Certificate as being something along the lines of a public policy program for current or future intelligence officers, to help them understand the full contours of the profession, how it works across its breadth, and relates to the U.S. Government writ large. The program provides students with an understanding of the ways in which the United States practices intelligence; the purposes to which it puts intelligence; the limits upon intelligence, be they practical, legal, ethical, or cultural; and the important debates in the field. The faculty members are scholars and practitioners with many years of experience in the field.

Dr. Brian Simpkins is the Associate Director of the Blue Grass State Intelligence Community Center of Academic Excellence (BGS IC CAE), at Eastern Kentucky University (EKU) in Richmond, KY. Brian Simpkins is also a part-time faculty member within the EKU Homeland Security Degree Program. The EKU Intelligence Studies Program is part of the Bachelor of Science in Homeland Security offered through the College of Justice and Safety. The Intelligence Studies Program started with a required intelligence process course for Homeland Security majors and then expanded to an interdisciplinary undergraduate Certificate in Intelligence Studies, requiring four courses to include intelligence history; intelligence process; counterintelligence; and intelligence analysis. It is paired with students completing four courses in a concentration, including intelligence collection and analysis; threat specialization; regional analysis (plus two language courses); security operations, and science and technology. EKU also offers a graduate Certificate in Intelligence and National Security with four courses in foundations of homeland security; terrorism and intelligence; intelligence analysis; and international relations. The undergraduate and graduate certificates are standalone in which a student can obtain the certificate without having to enroll or complete a formal degree. Starting in fall 2017, EKU will also offer a Minor in Cybersecurity and Intelligence pairing three intelligence courses in intelligence process; counterintelligence; and intelligence analysis; with four forensic computing courses.

Dr. Richard J. Kilroy, Jr., Assistant Professor of Politics at Coastal Carolina University (CCU) in Conway, SC, teaches intelligence analysis courses in support of CCU's Bachelor of Arts in Intelligence and National Security Studies (INTEL) degree program. The undergraduate intelligence degree program is administered within the Department of Politics at CCU, and as such, follows a traditional liberal arts curriculum. INTEL majors at CCU complete the University core curriculum, which includes foreign language; sciences; arts; politics; history; English; and math courses. Since students elect to be an INTEL major upon enrollment, they take courses during their core curriculum required for the major, to include anthropology; communications; geography; philosophy; and statistics. Foundational intelligence courses required for the major include Introduction to Intelligence Studies; Intelligence Communications; Intelligence Analysis; Intelligence Operations; Intelligence Research and Writing; and either Homeland Security or National Security. Students complete the program with a Capstone Course, which involves a major research paper. Students in other disciplines can also pursue a Minor in Intelligence and National Security Studies. Other minors available to INTEL majors include Geospatial Information Systems (GIS); Criminology; Global Studies; and Computer Science.

Discussion

The format of the roundtable discussion posed a series of questions on teaching Intelligence Analysis to each of the participants. The following is a summary of the responses from each of the faculty members.

1. What courses do you currently offer in Intelligence Analysis?

Stephen Coulthart stated that several courses are offered at UTEP, including Introduction to Intelligence Analysis; Intelligence Collection and Analysis; and Introduction to Intelligence and National Security course. Graduate-level courses are reading intensive, so students are expected to be familiar with most of the significant literature in the field of intelligence studies.

Brian Simpkins shared that EKU offers three upper level undergraduate courses which focus on intelligence analysis: HLS 321W Critical Problem Analysis (an undergraduate critical thinking course required for all Homeland Security majors); HLS 401 Intelligence Process; and HLS 403 Intelligence Analysis. At the graduate level, EKU offers HLS 825 Intelligence Analysis.

Sarah Miller Beebe explained that students pursuing JHU's Certificate in Intelligence are required to take one course in each of five areas: Introductory Courses; Theory; Operations; Law and Ethics; and Applications. The analysis course falls under the Operations requirement. It is also an elective in the various MA programs as well.

Since JMU's program is all about analysis, Stephen Marrin shared that there are 14 required courses in the Intelligence Analysis degree program: four courses focus on methods, how to think, counterfactuals, etc.; four courses focus on technology applications, such as data science, data mining, and visualization; and a number of others provide broad contextualization of the analytic function, as well as a senior Capstone course. In the Capstone course students conduct a self-initiated research plan, choose a topic and develop a research question, more along the lines of a senior thesis or self-initiated analytic product rather than one that was requested.

At CCU, Richard Kilroy explained that Intelligence Analysis is taught initially within the INTEL 200 Introduction to Intelligence Studies course, which students take in their freshman or sophomore year. Students later take INTEL 310 Intelligence Analysis as part of the major's foundational curriculum. Students can also take elective courses, such as POLI 399 Applied Intelligence Analysis and INTEL 337 Law Enforcement Intelligence, which teach intelligence analysis within the context of specific geopolitical regions, or disciplines.

2. Are your courses limited to Intelligence Studies majors only and what prerequisites are required for taking intelligence analysis courses?

Stephen Coulthart reiterated that at UTEP, only Intelligence Studies majors can take Intelligence Analysis courses. For Introduction to Intelligence Analysis and Intelligence Collection and Analysis, students need to take the Introduction to Intelligence and National Security course. This course provides a very broad overview of the field, to include the basic context of the intelligence community, the intelligence cycle, etc.

Brian Simpkins said that at EKU, any major may take the intelligence certificates or the new minor. The undergraduate certificate in particular was designed to be multidisciplinary to attract majors from across the campus. EKU is an Intelligence Community Center of Academic Excellence (IC CAE) and the IC CAE program office desires the multidisciplinary approach. EKU has been informed by the IC CAE program office that the IC desires graduates with degrees from a number of traditional academic disciplines, especially STEM degrees, who know something about intelligence and analysis. This is how the EKU Intelligence Studies Program was structured to provide students basic knowledge about intelligence and analysis paired with their traditional degree. There are no required undergraduate prerequisites for courses in intelligence analysis. It is recommended, however, that the student has taken the basic undergraduate research methods course in their major before enrolling in HLS 403 Intelligence Analysis.

Sarah Miller Beebe explained that intelligence analysis is fundamentally about understanding and communicating to decision makers what is known, not known, and surmised, as it can best be determined. Therefore, students in JHU's graduate degree programs will read seminal texts on intelligence analysis, discuss the complex cognitive, psychological, organizational, ethical, and legal issues surrounding intelligence analysis now and in the past, and apply analytic methodologies to real world problems. As a prerequisite for taking Intelligence Analysis, graduate students are expected to have completed one of the following: AS 470.620 Introduction to Intelligence in the Five Eyes Community; AS 470.711.51 Intelligence: From Secrets to Policy; or AS.470.748.51 The Art and Practice of Intelligence (or gain permission of instructor).

Stephen Marrin stated that at JMU, most courses in the IA program are limited to Intelligence Analysis majors, but he will take additional students who request to be added in. Since he is a Political Scientist by academic discipline in the multidisciplinary ISAT Department, Marrin noted that political science students who take IA courses seem to enjoy them and do well. As for prerequisite courses, the only requirement for students pursuing the BA in Intelligence Analysis is Statistics. For courses which Marrin teaches, functionally there are no prerequisites, since most are pitched as mid- to upper-level political science courses. Other courses in the Intelligence Analysis major do have prerequisites.

At CCU, due to the large number of students enrolled in the Intelligence and National Security Studies degree program (currently 350), Richard Kilroy explained that the Major Core required courses, such as Intelligence Analysis, are limited to INTEL majors or minors. To take the prerequisite course for all Major Core INTEL courses (INTEL 200 Introduction to Intelligence Studies), students are required to have taken POLI 201 American Government. Students must pass INTEL 200 with a grade of C or better if they are already a declared INTEL major. If they are an INTEL pre-major (determined by High School GPA and SAT/ACT test scores at admission), they must achieve a grade of B or better to become an INTEL major.

3. What pedagogical style do you use in teaching Intelligence Analysis? What course content do you include? What learning outcomes do you have for your students?

Stephen Coulthart shared that at UTEP, with undergraduates in his Intelligence Collection and Analysis course, he curates a classroom environment that is as interactive as possible. This is done to help keep students engaged. For example, he uses an exercise on HUMINT collection from Lahneman and Arcos (2014). In terms of content, he focuses on learning about intelligence analysis for 75 percent of the course (e.g., theory and substantive knowledge of intelligence agencies) and 25 percent on analytical skills (e.g., Bottom Line Up Front briefing and writing). The course content comes from two books. For the content on intelligence collection, he uses Lowenthal and Clark (2015) and for intelligence analysis content he uses Fingar (2011). In terms of intelligence analysis content, Coulthart expects that students walk away from the course being able to discuss and define intelligence analysis and how it fits into U.S. national security as well as identify the key issues and debates in intelligence analysis. To test for this knowledge he uses mostly multiple choice along with some short answers (one in class and one out of class). Coulthart's approach toward graduate intelligence analysis education is quite different from undergraduates. It is informed by Schon (1990), which stresses the importance of providing aspiring professionals with environments where they can fail, adopt, and succeed repeatedly. In developing his syllabus for the course, he drew inspiration from art studios where students are given difficult tasks and allowed to "fumble" through them. Coulthart sees his role in this course less as an instructor imparting knowledge and more as a coach/resource person helping students make sense of each task. In terms of learning outcomes he expects that students will possess a basic understanding of the context of intelligence analysis (e.g., historical and organizational) and basic intelligence analysis proficiencies (e.g., searching, validating, organizing, analyzing, and communicating).

Brian Simpkins explained that at EKU, each of the courses which cover intelligence analysis employ different pedagogies determined by the expected learning outcomes. For example, HLS 321W Critical Process, on-campus, utilizes a lecture and lab format—each week has a lecture on the assigned topic and students then are provided exercises or team simulations where they must use the material covered in the lecture as they work on a major research project. The online version of HLS 321W is a self-study course where the students do the same simulations and exercises as on-campus students and also develop a major research project. The course utilizes Elder and Paul's (2016) framework from the *Thinker's Guide to Analytic Thinking*. The last four to five weeks of HLS 401 Intelligence Process, which focuses on intelligence analysis, employs a team-based learning format on-campus, and online a self-study format. HLS 403 Intelligence Analysis employs a seminar format with extensive case study work done individually and in teams. The online course is more self-study, but still employs student team projects. HLS 825 Intelligence Analysis is only taught online and is done in a self-study format with significant case study work done by individual students and an individual student threat analysis project. Intelligence analysis courses utilize a number of techniques from Heuer and Pherson (2014), to include Analysis of Competing Hypotheses (ACH); What If Analysis; Red Teaming; and Indicators Analysis. The course also uses Clark (2016), based on formal modeling and case studies.

Sarah Miller Beebe shared her teaching pedagogy at JHU, which includes learning objectives, multiple learning methods, and assessment types. The graduate intelligence analysis course she teaches is designed to ensure that it fits within the curriculum, includes clearly defined terminal learning objectives and multiple, relevant assessment methods. There is a strong critical thinking and metacognitive underpinning to the course. She structures her teaching as a seminar to guide graduate students through the 14-week course. It is literature-based with learning objectives for every class meeting and opportunities throughout the semester to bridge theory and practice. She employs readings from a number of sources, to include George and Bruce (2014), Heuer and Pherson (2014), Beebe and Pherson (2014), Clark (2016), National Research Council (2011), DNI (2015), and CIA (2009). She also recommends that students read historical literature such as Kent (1949).

Stephen Marrin reiterated that since JMU's program is all about analysis, the faculty members in the program employ a variety of pedagogical styles in teaching different courses. For his knowledge-based courses, he recognizes the challenge in teaching undergraduates that they do not often read the assigned materials. Therefore, he assigns papers that have the following as a requirement: answer a question by referencing key content from each of the assigned readings into a holistic, synthetic evaluation of the course content. This provides a platform for the students to develop their evaluative and argumentative skills (the core skills of the strategic intelligence analyst). Marrin also has students prepare strategic intelligence assessments in a capstone course. Students in this course can choose a client for whom they will present their paper as the consumer of the product, or they can produce it as a self-initiated product. Since this is a two semester course process, students must pick a topic, choose a research question, identify methods to employ, and then implement the research design by learning in a trial and error way (like riding a bike), where they continually revise their research design and ultimate product. Marrin stated that his goals as a political scientist teaching social context in an intelligence analysis program are to (1) give students knowledge about aspects of intelligence, intelligence analysis, and national security decision making; (2) be diagnostic and give the students a chance to decide if national security intelligence analysis (or intelligence, or analysis, or national security) is the right path for them; and (3) be preparatory, or as Rob Johnson (2005) referred to it, a kind of "sociological acculturation" ... a preparation for what it takes to do analysis well. Marrin said that JMU's Intelligence Analysis program is very much like the new pre-med degree programs, which go beyond science education to now include a multidisciplinary approach which includes a social context (e.g., including courses in philosophy, psychology, and sociology), with the goal being a solid knowledge foundation for those who choose to go to medical school after graduation. He says the JMU intelligence analysis program has many similarities with this pre-med approach to undergraduate education (Marrin 2009).

At CCU, Richard Kilroy explained that multiple faculty teach INTEL 310 Intelligence Analysis and each brings in their own pedagogy to enhance learning. In the Introductory course, INTEL 200, however, where students are first exposed to Intelligence Analysis, all faculty use Jensen, McElreath, and Graves (2012). In his INTEL 310 classes, Kilroy begins by discussing critical thinking using literature such as Heuer (1999); Moore (2007); and Facione (2015). The course then focuses on teaching Structured Analytical Techniques (SAT), using Heuer and Pherson's (2014) text, along with Beebe and Pherson (2014). Students work in teams assigned to specific case studies, which then must "teach" the other students in the class about the case study, guide them through the use of the appropriate SAT, and then demonstrate an understanding of the SAT by explaining their outcome. As a culmination of the course, students also work in teams to analyze a contemporary security situation by developing four scenarios for the possibility of a Third Intifada in the Middle East, using adversarial collaboration and structured debate to argue their most likely outcome. In addition to the written papers, the assessment instruments for the course include a midterm which is more objective (multiple choice, true/false, short answer) assessing Bloom's lower cognitive skills and a final exam (all essay questions) assessing Bloom's higher cognitive skills (Bloom 1956).

Questions from the Audience

At the conclusion of the discussion, the roundtable participants took questions from the audience.

One question focused on teaching students the importance of getting a security clearance and how to do that. Stephen Coulthart mentioned that at UTEP, they cover this in their new student orientation, given the prevalence of social media today and how public students are with their personal lives. Brian Simpkins stated that at EKU, students are taught how to be smart about getting a clearance in their JSO 100 course. They learn about background checks, medical issues, financial disclosures (paying rent on time, etc.). Further, the BGS IC CAE and homeland security student groups often bring in guest speakers who discuss the security clearance process. Richard Kilroy said that at CCU, in their National Security Club, students are taught about filling out an SF 86 (starting now to gather information needed from parents, employers, etc.).

Another question was: is it alright for students to fail? Stephen Marrin argued that yes it is, since it is acceptable to try something and learn from experiences. In the capstone project he does not grade solely on the quality of the final project, but also on the degree to which the students engage with the learning experience as well as a reflective essay at the end of the process. This reflective essay, modeled on a paper the graduate students at Brunel University's MA in Intelligence and Security Studies write at the end of the Brunel Analytic Simulation Exercise (BASE), allows students to reflect on the process, have good conversations on failure and recovery, and understand how lessons learned help prevent future failures.

One question addressed whether students are exposed to courses in philosophy and logic at the different schools. Stephen Coulthart said that undergraduate UTEP students do take these courses as part of the Liberal Arts core curriculum. For graduate courses, students learn methods of argumentation. Stephen Marrin stated that at JMU students do learn critical thinking skills in their methods courses which were developed and taught by Noel Hendrickson based on his background in philosophy (Hendrickson 2008). Richard Kilroy shared that at CCU, Intelligence majors are required to take PHIL 110, Introduction to Logic, as part of their Intelligence Foundation curriculum.

A student from the University of Mississippi provided a brief overview of the Intelligence Studies program at Ole Miss, which does not offer an Intelligence major, but rather a minor in Intelligence to compliment other majors. Students take six courses in Intelligence Studies, to include Analytics I and II, where they must score a B or higher. In these courses they learn Structured Analytical Techniques, how to brief and write effectively, using estimative language in the intelligence community. Ole Miss also requires students to have had an internship during their undergraduate studies, which provides a career-oriented sense of purpose to the program of study.

A lecturer at Edith Cowan University in Perth, Australia asked about how faculty in the United States develop assessment tasks for intelligence analysis courses. Stephen Coulthart stated that in his graduate intelligence analysis course, they have four modules in their course which include the context of intelligence analysis (e.g., socio-organizational issues); setting analysis (e.g., requirement analysis); methods of analysis (e.g., forecasting and hypothesis testing); and analytical communication (e.g., writing and briefing). He also stated that his research informs his teaching and helps determine methods of assessment. For example, his doctoral thesis at the University of Pittsburgh focused on the effectiveness of Structured Analytical Techniques in intelligence analysis. New information has been discovered on the use of SATs, in regards to what works and what does not (Coulthart 2017). Sarah Miller Beebe uses multiple assessment instruments in her graduate courses at JHU which demonstrate logic and reasoning as they read the intelligence analysis literature. Students produce short reaction papers, complete analytic problem sets, provide oral briefings, and produce an annotated bibliography and longer paper on a topic relating to intelligence analysis. Throughout the semester-long seminar they engage in give-and-take discussions focused on class-generated key questions that align with the learning objectives for each week. Beebe used the example of solving a math problem, where students not only study the literature, including theory and methods (like SATs), but also "show the work" of their analysis—a process that helps them bridge theory and practice and observe their own intellectual progress. Richard Kilroy shared that at CCU, there are assessments within courses tied to the learning objectives, but there are also program assessments required by the university. For Intelligence Studies, there is not a formal test, such as a major field exam like other majors (Political Science, for example). He suggested that maybe this is something that IAFIE could help develop.

Conclusion

Since the roundtable was limited to 70 minutes, there were more topics that were left for another discussion, as well as questions that did not get asked. In the end, the roundtable left the "tale as old as time" of whether intelligence analysis is an art or science open to further dialog (Landon-Murray and Coulthart 2016). The good news is that academics and practitioners are talking to each other, and in many schools, teaching together. This ultimately benefits students who desire to pursue careers as intelligence analysts by having faculty members who bring diverse experiences throughout the intelligence community as practitioners, along with academics and scholars who bring new research into analytical methodologies, new pedagogies, and new insights into teaching intelligence analysis.

Acknowledgements

I wish to thank Dr. Larry Valero, UTEP, for his support in adding this roundtable discussion to the IAFIE conference.

References

Ashman, Howard, and Alen Menken. 1991. "Original Song Lyrics for Beauty and the Beast." MetroLyrics. http://www.metrolyrics.com/beauty-and-the-beast-lyrics-disney.html

Beebe, Sarah Miller, and Randy Pherson. 2014. *Cases in Intelligence Analysis: Structured Analytic Techniques in Action*. 2nd ed. Washington, DC: CQ Press.

Bloom, Benjamin S., ed. 1956. *Taxonomy of Educational Objectives, Handbook I: The Cognitive Domain*. New York: David McKay Co., Inc.

CIA. 2009. *CIA Tradecraft Primer*. https://www.cia.gov/library/center-for-the-study-of-intelligence/csi-publications/books-and-monographs/TradecrafPrimer-apr09.pdf

Clark, Robert. 2016. *Intelligence Analysis: A Target-Centric Approach.* 5th ed. Washington, DC: CQ Press.

Coulthart, Stephen. 2017. "An Evidence-Based Evaluation of 12 Core Structured Analytic Techniques." *International Journal of Intelligence and Counter Intelligence* 30 (2): 368–391. doi:10.1080/08850607.2016.1230706.

DNI. 2015. *ICD 203 Analytical Standards.* DNI Office of the Director of Intelligence Analysis. https://www.dni.gov/files/documents/ICD/ICD 203 Analytic Standards.pdf.

Elder, Linda, and Richard Paul. 2016. *Thinker's Guide to Analytic Thinking.* Tomales, CA: Foundation for Critical Thinking.

Facione, Peter. 2015. "Critical Thinking: What It Is and Why It Counts." *Insight Assessment.* http://citeseerx.ist.psu.edu/viewdoc/d?doi=10.1.1.829.1794&rep=rep1&type=pdf

Fingar, Thomas. 2011. *Reducing Uncertainty: Intelligence Analysis and National Security.* Palo Alto, CA: Stanford Security Studies.

George, Roger, and James Bruce, ed. 2014. *Analyzing Intelligence: National Security Practitioners' Perspectives.* 2nd ed. Washington, DC: Georgetown University Press.

Hendrickson, Noel. 2008. "Critical Thinking in Intelligence Analysis." *International Journal of Intelligence and Counterintelligence* 21 (4): 679–693. doi:10.1080/08850600802254749.

Heuer, Jr. Richards. 1999. *Psychology of Intelligence Analysis.* Washington, DC: Center for the Study of Intelligence.

Heuer, Jr. Richards, and Randy Pherson. 2014. *Structured Analytical Techniques for Intelligence Analysis.* 2nd ed. Washington, DC: CQ Press.

Jensen, Carl, David McElreath, and Melissa Graves. 2012. *Introduction to Intelligence Studies.* Boca Raton, FL: CRC Press.

Johnson, Rob. 2005. *Analytic Culture in the U.S. Intelligence Community: An Ethnographic Study.* Washington, DC: Center for the Study of Intelligence.

Kent, Sherman. 1949. *Strategic Intelligence for American World Policy*. Princeton, NJ: Princeton University Press.

Lahneman, William, and Ruben Arcos. 2014. *The Art of Intelligence: Simulations, Exercises, and Games*. New York: Rowan and Littlefield.

Landon-Murray, Michael, and Stephen Coulthart. 2016. "Academic Intelligence Programs in the United States: Exploring the Training and Tradecraft Debate." *Global Security and Intelligence Studies* 2 (1): Article 3: 2–19. doi:10.18278/gsis. 2.1.2.

Lowenthal, Mark. 2016. *Intelligence: From Secrets to Policy*. 7th ed. Washington, DC: CQ Press.

Lowenthal, Mark, and Robert Clark. 2015. *The 5 Disciplines of Intelligence Collection*. Washington, DC: CQ Press.

Marrin, Stephen. 2009. "Training and Educating U.S. Intelligence Analysts." *International Journal of Intelligence and Counter Intelligence* 22 (1): 131–146. doi:10.1080/08850600802486986.

Moore, David. 2007. *Critical Thinking and Intelligence Analysis*. Washington, DC: National Defense Intelligence College.

National Research Council. 2011. *Intelligence Analysis for Tomorrow: Advances from the Behavioral and Social Sciences*. Committee on Behavioral and Social Science Research to Improve Intelligence Analysis for National Security, Board on Behavioral, Cognitive, and Sensory Sciences, Division of Behavioral and Social Sciences and Education. Washington, DC: National Academies Press.

Schon, Donald. 1990. *Educating the Reflective Practitioner: Toward a New Design for Teaching and Learning in the Professions*. San Francisco, CA: Jossey-Bass.

Review of *Relentless Strike: The Secret History of Joint Special Operations Command*

Sean Naylor (2015). *Relentless Strike: The Secret History of Joint Special Operations Command*. New York: St. Martin's Press. ISBN: 978-1-250-01454-2 (Hbk), 978-1-4668-7622-4 (Ebk). 540 pages. $29.99

Like credible intelligence nonfiction, attempts to probe into the sensitive world of contemporary Special Operations Forces (SOF) activity provide numerous, often impenetrable, challenges for authors attempting to write factually accurate portrayals of such clandestine capabilities. However, from time to time, good writers with good access, good sources, and a little luck are able to piece together intricate and disparate sources to penetrate the veils of secrecy and operational security; Sean Naylor's *Relentless Strike: The Secret History of Joint Special Operations Command* is one such publication.

The Joint Special Operations Command (JSOC) is the coordinating body for America's premier Special Forces units; it includes the Army's Delta Force, the Navy's SEALs, and the Air Force's Special Operations Aviation Regiment. Naylor takes the reader on a journey that chronologically maps the evolutionary history of the Command, from the failed Iranian hostage rescue attempt in 1980, to the invasion of Grenada in 1983, to Panama and Manuel Noriega's capture in 1989, to Desert Storm, Bosnia, Afghanistan, and Iraq. Naylor intricately weaves lesser known rescues, renditions, and other direct action operations throughout the volume, in addition to the most well-known of all, the death of al-Qaeda leader Osama Bin Laden in 2011.

The author's research comes from a variety of sources including official documents, open-source/publicly available material, as well as a significant number of interviews with JSOC operators and commanders. Ten years earlier, Naylor had penned *Not A Good Day to Die* which chronicled his experiences as a reporter for the United States Army Times, where he was embedded with US forces during key periods of Operation ANACONDA, the first large-scale military action to involve large numbers of US conventional forces, as well as SOF. During this deployment, Naylor was able to interview a number of Special Forces participants, and clearly, these relationships developed and expanded, and have assisted immeasurably in *Relentless Strike*.

Relentless Strike is a dense text but it is not an academic volume. It captures the rise and evolution of JSOC without considering the overall strategic considerations that may have seen this expansion come about. The successful evolution of JSOC has much to do with operational successes post-Operation EAGLE CLAW in 1980, as well as the strengths of personalities in command of these forces, especially those who have demonstrated the very necessary political—strategic—savvy to be able to influence policymakers. This Naylor clearly illustrates; strength of personality in the shape of William McRaven, Mike Flynn, and Stanley McChrystal reflects prominent individuals who dominate the narrative, particularly throughout the second half of the volume, and are at the forefront of JSOC's progression. In *Relentless Strike*, Naylor shows us that despite JSOC having always regarded itself as much more than a specialized, precision "blunt-force" tool used to crack especially "hard-nuts," it now appears to have successfully convinced policymakers of this also.

So, might the same SF—National Security nexus be presenting itself in Canada, the United Kingdom, Australia, or New Zealand? While Naylor's book focuses solely on the United States example, *Relentless Strike* may, in fact, give us a glimpse into how the "Five-Eyes" SOF community has evolved over the last decade and a half. Naylor specifically considers the expansion of SEAL TEAM 6 and how in the space of 10 years the unit expanded from less than 500 "to more than 1500, of whom only about 300 were SEALs, with the rest consisting of roughly 800 other uniformed Navy personnel and about 400 civilians who together provided administration, intelligence, logistics, communications, and other support." Even the smallest member of the "Five Eyes" SOF community—New Zealand's Special Operations Forces (NZSOF) has over the last 10 years quietly expanded their capabilities, roles, functions and, one might suggest, influence. Not only is there now a New Zealand SAS Regiment, an aspiration that was less than 30 years earlier regarded as a "pipe-dream" by one former senior SAS officer, NZDF's SOC now coordinates NZSOF up to the highest levels of government, directly linked to the wider national security command authority. This is what we now see in Canada, the United Kingdom, and Australia, which in many ways mirrors Naylor's description of the rise of JSOC.

For those interested in the evolution of SOFs and military intelligence—both collection and analysis—*Relentless Strike* offers insights into how this has begun to be transformed in the twenty-first century. From the use of Predator drones' "Unblinking eye" constant surveillance, to the clandestine installation of cyber café keystroke recognition software, the startling array of intelligence capability now possessed by JSOC units tells us something of the importance of intelligence and the desire to have an independent capability rather than be reliant on traditional partner agencies for such support. If we read Naylor's book, one could argue that JSOC's solution to the intelligence challenges has been to create its very own collection and analysis capability; SIGINT, HUMINT, surveillance expertise that was once the sole bastion of the likes of CIA and NSA is now firmly part of the US SOF machinery.

This particular evolution begs the question, how might the rest of a National Security infrastructure feel about such developments? There are a number of examples within *Relentless Strike* where the CIA clearly relied on JSOC to assist with operations—particularly in the early stages of Operation Enduring Freedom in Afghanistan. If there is indeed political support for such an evolution of force in the United States, then is this development being mirrored around the world in other countries? One wonders whether others within the international Special Forces community have similarly followed suit and established dedicated intelligence collection and analysis capability beyond that which their traditional intelligence community partners have provided previously.

Relentless Strike offers an opportunity to understand the genesis of the United States' twenty-first century Special Operations, and as such gives us some insight into the key operational deliverables available to American National Security policymakers, and even those other key members of what has become the international Special Forces global network. The painstaking detail, multiple, cross-referenced sourcing is commendable, and makes for a considerable, and thoroughly enjoyable, volume.

Dr. Rhys Ball

Lecturer at Massey University's Centre for Defence and Security Studies (CDSS), Auckland, New Zealand

His 2009 doctoral thesis examined New Zealand Special Forces operations during the Vietnam War

Review of *Why America Misunderstands the World: National Experience and Roots of Misperception*

Paul R. Pillar (2016). *Why America Misunderstands the World: National Experience and Roots of Misperception*. New York: Columbia University Press. ISBN: 9780231165907 (Hbk), 9780231540353 (Ebk). 224 pages. $29.95

This is a very perceptive study of the roots of American foreign policy. Notice the book's title is not "Does America Misunderstand the World?"; it is a forgone conclusion that the majority of Americans and consequently our politicians misunderstand foreigners' perceptions of Americans and American foreign policy. Former veteran CIA agent and academic Paul R. Pillar focuses on "American exceptionalism" and its resultant effect on Americans' perceptions of foreigners and their unique circumstances.

This book contributes to the genre of foreign relations as both a correction and an explanation. Pillar admits its message is "unavoidably downbeat" (x), however it is not consciously anti-American but instead seeks to enhance accurate perception through the virtues of knowing oneself and consequently knowing others more correctly.

The literature of American foreign policy and intelligence studies is replete with examples of "intelligence failures." In this perceptive volume on perception itself, Pillar demonstrates that American foreign policy decisions are not made based on the advice of the Intelligence Community typically but are the products of Americans' gross misperceptions of foreigners and their interests. Americans' heuristics, shaped by beneficial geography since the nation's inception and an unparalleled record of success culminating in the status as the world's lone superpower, drive Americans to view the world not as it is but through a prism of distortion. Pillar believes this misperception, based on a belief in American exceptionalism and a monolithic view of the rest of the world, has led to such foreign policy "blunders" as the Iraq War. Following Pillar's 2014 book *Intelligence and U.S. Foreign Policy: Iraq, 9/11, and Misguided Reform*, this book serves as a correction to misplaced blame.

Because the United States was insulated from foreign conflicts and seemingly permanent border disputes by virtue of its position between two oceans and because it rapidly evolved into not only a land of prosperity but also the world's lone superpower, Americans project their experience on foreigners without questioning the vast differences in circumstances. Americans believe themselves to be exceptional and their national interests benign and have no conception of foreign rejection of these concepts.

Pillar convincingly argues this thesis as well as the necessary (from the intelligence analyst's point of view) argument that American foreign policy is not rooted in sound intelligence work, but rather in the preconceptions of ideology of American decision makers. Foreign policy has historically been chaotic because it has typically been subordinated to domestic politics.

Americans are typically guilty of gross oversimplification of foreign countries and global dynamics generally. Pillar demonstrates this claim with the example of the George W. Bush Administration's monolithic view of terrorists and nations which did not support his worldview. It is a "for us or against us" attitude that led to the "blunder" that was the Iraq War.

This monograph's sole weakness lies in Pillar's argument and overall tone in his unequivocal rejection of neoconservative ideology and politicians over other foreign policy influences, foreign or domestic. Pillar unequivocally condemns present-day American neoconservatism as an insidious force which harnesses the misperception resulting from American national experience and projects its ideology as an unnecessarily confrontational crusade to universally apply what it considers "American values." Hindsight may condemn recent American military action as a "glaring and still recent blunder" (163), yet neither the American invasions of Afghanistan or Iraq would have happened without the 9/11 attacks—motivated by Osama bin Laden's own ideological and provincial desire to rid the Middle East of American influence by initiating a holy war.

Furthermore, he excoriates neoconservatives for their "pathological loathing of Presidents Bill Clinton and Barack Obama" (174), but I did not find a corresponding condemnation of Democrats and their media sycophants for their vitriol against President George W. Bush, particularly in his second term. Pillar even sides with the Hillary Clinton camp on the Benghazi hearings, which he terms "exploitation" (174), not a search for the truth after a campaign of lies and stonewalling. This type of bias mars, for me anyway, a very perceptive book (on perception).

Although this book was released in May 2016 and therefore before the presidential election, it is even timelier due to the seismic shift in foreign policy expected with the transition from the idealist Obama Administration to the populist Trump's. Pillar opines the need for a "dialogue" in the United States as a path toward a better understanding of the interaction between the United States and the rest of the world rather than the partisan rancor which more often worsens American misperception. In his conclusion, Pillar holds out hope for American leaders who will actually lead—not simply follow the misguided commonly held assumptions of the herd. Based on his own evidence however, this would require a seismic shift in the dominant American perception of the world.

Clinton L. Ervin

American Public University System

Review of *The Handbook of European Intelligence Cultures*

Bob de Graaff and James N. Nyce, with Chelsea Locke (eds.) (2016). *The Handbook of European Intelligence Cultures.* Rowman & Littlefield Publishers. 2016. ISBN: 978-1-4422-4941-7. 496 pages. £75.00

The growth of intelligence studies in the Western world is a reality, not only in the Anglo-Saxon world, but also in continental Europe where scholars seek a broader understanding of an increasingly important discipline that is still not very well known, mostly being developed as one specific dimension of security studies. One may consider that times are changing and intelligence is fitting not only into the center of some social sciences, but also into public opinion after its mediatization in the political arena with the Snowden scandal, due to its "inefficiency" in preventing terrorist attacks in New York, Washington, Bali, Madrid, London, Bombay, Paris, or Berlin and at the same time by allowing a controversial military intervention in Iraq. If these facts were not enough, we may also consider the increasing importance of intelligence in the business world where competitive intelligence plays a major role in helping a company develop a competitive advantage in an increasingly global marketplace full of competition. Thus, there are many reasons why intelligence studies are developing very fast, opening space to create an autonomous discipline much needed in a complex and uncertain world.

Handbook of European Intelligence Cultures is part of the Security and Professional Intelligence Education Series (SPIES) edited by Jan Goldman since 2008 and looks at intelligence through a security perspective, but goes further because it aims to approach intelligence cultures. One of the book's main ideas is that national intelligence cultures depend on each country's history and security environment, though are influenced not only by a broader political culture of the country, but also by other countries' models. Taking into consideration EU member states (except Cyprus, Hungary, Latvia, and Malta) and eight other European countries (Albania, Bosnia and Herzegovina, Iceland, Montenegro, Norway, Serbia, Switzerland, and Ukraine) this book intends to give readers some insight about almost unknown intelligence communities as well as little-known national intelligence agencies. So, it allows the reader to explore both long seen intelligence systems as in the United Kingdom or France and some latecomers such as Montenegro or Eastern European countries. This volume is edited by Bob de Graaf and James M. Nyce; the former with many insightful publications in intelligence studies since the beginning of the last decade and the latter with a very strong path in military intelligence, with Chelsea Locke. Looking at the title, it gives the reader some hints about what he/she is going to find out in this volume, which is a detailed handbook that all intelligence scholars must have on their bookshelves, especially because it not only characterizes very efficiently each country's intelligence system, but also refers to existing differences among intelligence cultures inside Europe instead of a common and shared European intelligence culture.

The book is organized as one chapter for each country (32 chapters arranged alphabetically) with an introduction authored by de Graaf and Nyce where the authors let the readers know the purpose of this book and why it is needed in a moment of growing studies in this relatively new field of study. They present the framework of analysis suggested to every country's contributor to follow, though it is not always strictly followed. Some authors address many of these common topics while others do not, instead applying their own analysis. Though it does not weaken the volume as whole, it presents challenges to the reader due to different approaches followed by the 38 contributors, whether reinforcing a more historical description or a more analytical view based on law or organizational changes. In addition, the authors go through different time periods of analysis in different chapters, which in the end makes sense since the political history of each country is also quite different. Having said that, there is another good and probably unintended contribution from this volume concerning the references. Every contributor uses secondary sources complementing the information they obtained from the agencies' websites or from national laws, which allows further reading and some main references for each country.

There are two main reasons why this book creates an additional value when compared to previous similar attempts like the 2003 volume *"Democracy, Law and Security: Internal Security Services in Contemporary Europe,"* edited by Jean-Paul Brodeur, Peter Gill, and Dennis Töllborg; the two volumes of the *"PSI Handbook of Global Security and Intelligence,"* published in 2008 and edited by Stuart Farson, Peter Gill, Mark Phythian, and Shlomo Shpiro; and the 2013 *"Intelligence Elsewhere,"* edited by Philip H.J. Davies and Kristian Gustafson. The first reason is the enlargement in case studies since this volume explores 32 different countries and focus on each country's intelligence community instead of just a single agency, allowing the reader to understand the full national intelligence system which includes both civil and military intelligence agencies. Secondly is the effort to make a comprehensive and systematic approach using an outlined framework that focuses both on the impact of environmental factors and internal factors from the community or the organization itself, helping the authors to explore a similar path in each chapter and giving the reader some hints to make meaningful comparisons.

The only main criticism is that there is not any conclusion about common and different paths across time and space and if we may be going through a Europeanization of intelligence cultures inside Europe due to the need to share information (both nationally and internationally). Despite the efforts to sum up some big conclusions in the Introduction, it does not go very deep on how different critical junctures as World War II, democratization, the end of the Cold War or terrorism, especially after 9/11, led to both similar and different organizational changes. However, it is understandable that the book does not go this way because one of its goals is to allow others to make those comparisons. Therefore, it is a major contribution to political scientists, historians, sociologists, and other academics as well as to intelligence practitioners around the world because it allows them to understand how intelligence is carried out in European countries.

João Estevens

Portuguese Institute of International Relations
Nova University of Lisbon, Portugal

www.ingramcontent.com/pod-product-compliance
Lightning Source LLC
Chambersburg PA
CBHW081648270326
41933CB00018B/3396